BATCHED & BOTTLED

CONTENTS

INTRODUCTION

Why batch and bottle cocktails? Because it's hands down the best way to plan ahead, to reduce work at times when you want to be relaxing, and to have something delicious waiting for you at the very moment you'd like it. Preparing a cocktail in advance just makes sense: when the time comes that you actually want to be drinking or entertaining, it can be as straightforward as grabbing a few glasses and pouring the chilled liquid from the bottle.

But batching and bottling isn't just about practicality. It allows for some cocktail flair. Our French 75, for example (p64), is best served from a champagne bottle – with a neatly written label and a bit of theatre from the server (i.e. you), your guests will feel like they're somewhere far more glamourous than your living room. At our bar, Three Sheets in Dalston, London, we think that any preparation that can be done ahead is for the benefit of the guests. And the same applies to you at home. As a good friend once put it: 'You wouldn't start cooking a dinner for a party when your guests arrive.'

You'll notice we've divided the book into chapters based on seasons. That's because we believe drinking, just like eating, is best if you follow nature, and match what you're making to what's going on outside. Just as a light, spritzy drink is more appealing in the sunshine, so a rich, comforting drink feels like just what we want when the nights draw in. Some of the recipes we've shared are ideal for a long, lazy afternoon in the park with a picnic (like the refreshing and fragrant Sencha Collins, p24), others are just perfect for a quiet night in with a loved one (and they'll love you even more if you make them a Fig Negroni, p128).

We also want to introduce you to interesting cocktail-making techniques like carbonating, fat-washing, clarification and fermentation, but we've stayed away from using expensive scientific-type equipment, as we know that only a very small proportion of people have access to it. In fact, many of the recipes are as easy as combining a few ingredients in a bottle (like the Yuzu Negroni, p124), though some are a bit more elaborate but very rewarding (try our Malts, Oats & Leaf, p130, flavoured with manuka tincture and served from a soda siphon). If you want to start somewhere simple, we recommend you check out the Hidden Martini (p132), 15 Second Old Fashioned (p156) and the Wedding Hip Flask (p126). For something a little more technical, yet still straightforward, try the Whisky Soda (p146), or get into one of the recipes that involves fermentation: it's fun and super-addictive, but you may, like us, end up with cupboards full of resting fruit and bubbling liquids, which doesn't always go down too well with the other halves.

We also want our recipes to be adaptable. Everyone has their own tastes, so we've tried to include flavour alternatives in recipes. If you're not keen on the nettle cordial in the Foraged Martini (see p68), say, we've suggested you try swapping it for elderflower or dandelion. The same applies to some of the techniques. Once you have fat-washed the whisky for the Scottish Coffee (p182), you can do it to any spirit you like, from rum to gin.

Throughout the book you'll notice a few recipes from some of our close friends from around the world. We really believe that the best way to learn and progress is through conversation and collaboration. We've been lucky to cross paths with some of the brightest and most determined people in our industry, and we couldn't resist the chance to get them involved (although when we tried their drinks, we were a little worried the guys might show us up). Massive thanks to Marcis, Nathan, Hyacinthe, Luke and Alex for their contributions. They are at the top of their games, and they know that working with seasonal ingredients and batching is the way forward for anyone who makes drinks.

We both hope you enjoy the drinks in this book. The recipes are a truly tasty starting point from which you can go on to experiment. And hopefully the stunning photography is an inspiration too. We wanted to show the drinks honestly, so that when you make them at home they look the same as ours: not over-stylised, no fake ice.

I think the biggest reason for us to put our ideas onto paper was to dispel the myth that you need a bunch of expensive equipment and years of experience to make top-quality drinks. With a little knowledge and basic kitchen items, you can produce stunning cocktails at home that are really easy to serve.

ABOUT US

We are brothers. We're Northern lads who grew up in Manchester, which has definitely had an impact on our style of hospitality. We are firm believers that everyone should be welcome at our bar and that's why we enjoyed opening it in east London, with its rich history and character. Both of us slipped into bartending as a consequence of going to university. Max used bartending to help with finances while studying in Edinburgh. I got into bartending when university didn't pan out as expected. We also both worked at the same local boozer in Manchester to earn some extra cash. It was a real salt-of-the-earth place: no frills, lots of spills and a fair few bellyaches.

We'll introduce each other: it's probably the only time we'll ever say anything nice about each other in print, so I guess this one's for you, Mum.

NOEL *by Max*

He started his career, properly, in Manchester, after messing around for a few years with uni. Noel has a strong grasp on what's important in a bar: keeping people happy, and looking at the bigger picture; music, lighting and mood is what makes people come back. Hopefully this book shows that drinks can be pretty easy to get right, but creating a good atmosphere is something you need a talent for, and he gets it, in his own grumpy way.

MAX *by Noel*

Max started working in bars in Edinburgh at a hotel called Rick's. He then moved back to Manchester after finishing university and continued his journey into the cocktail world at some of the city's best bars. He was one of the top bartenders who worked at the legendary Socio Rehab. He then moved to London to work at the inimitable 69 Colebrooke Row under industry great Tony Conigliaro. As I've started to learn, he's always trying to sod off for a few days on a 'work' trip: he's had opportunities to travel pretty extensively, experiencing the global drinks and food industry, which was valuable when we were trying to figure out what to do with our own bar.

It was early 2016 when Max called me with the idea of opening our own place in London. I said yes almost instantly. It moved forward rapidly – let's just say we begged and borrowed to scrape together the money – and six months later Three Sheets was open. And now we wouldn't change a thing.

EQUIPMENT & TECHNIQUES

We've tried to keep the equipment used as everyday as possible, and only listed the more unusual items. We haven't included household basics such as cling film (plastic wrap), pans and knives. Everyone has those, right?

BLENDER A top-loading jug is better than a stick blender, as it processes more evenly.

COFFEE FILTERS These are essential when straining off ingredients in various recipes. You might find smaller, 'one-cup'-sized filters in the supermarket, but they don't hold much liquid at a time – the bigger ones are better. Your local specialist coffee shop will probably stock them. For more on this, see Straining (p12).

COOKING THERMOMETER Essential for when you're heating liquids to infuse flavours. Alcohol boils at 78°C/172°F, so keeping under that is key to making sure the recipes work. Digital thermometers are easier to read and more accurate.

DIGITAL SCALES Probably our most-used bit of kit when prepping ingredients in the bar. We would recommend buying one that can weigh up to 3kg/6½lbs with one decimal place.

ELECTRIC JUICER Centrifugal juicers are great for extracting juice from fruits such as apples and other ingredients such as ginger.

EMPTY GLASS BOTTLES For storing your cocktails, there is nothing better. There are shops where you can buy them empty, but we would always recommend reusing bottles. Once you've finished a bottle of wine, gin or other spirit, keep the cap or cork and soak off the label. Before you fill it with your delicious homemade cocktail, it's vital to sterilise it, if the cocktail contains fruit juice or another fresh ingredient. Do this with a sterilising agent bought from a chemist or homebrew supplier, or with heat: wash the bottles in hot, soapy water and bake in a preheated oven (140°C/280°F/Gas Mark 1) until dry. Bottled cocktails and cordials should always be sealed.

FUNNELS Obviously useful for getting liquid into a bottle, but also very handy for straining off solids. Funnels support coffee filters perfectly.

JIGGERS/MEASURES These are ideal for adding volumes of liquid under 100ml/4oz. Most supermarkets now stock them.

KILNER JARS OR SIMILAR These are great for storing liquid. They are also amazing for fermenting fruit, as they are easy to release pressure from. Having a few is always handy. You can use an alternative container, but it must be made of a non-reactive material (i.e. glass or plastic) and have a tight-fitting lid. They should be sterilised before use with either a sterilising agent bought from a chemist or homebrew supplier, or with heat: wash them in hot, soapy water and bake in a preheated oven (140°C/280°F/Gas Mark 1) until they're dry. If they have rubber seals, take those off and boil them separately – the hot oven will damage them.

MEASURING JUGS Having a range of sizes, from large to small, helps with making batches of drinks.

MEASURING SPOONS These are very handy if you want to add small amounts of potent ingredients to large batches.

MUDDLING In bars we use a little tool called a muddler to gently crush ingredients, but at home you can use a rolling pin or pestle.

PIPETTE It's what we use for adding very small volumes of liquid, such as orange flower water, to drinks. But a teaspoon or measuring spoon will work.

CARBONATING

Carbonation is what makes things fizzy, and it happens when carbon dioxide (CO_2) is dissolved into liquid under pressure. When pressure is released (i.e. a cap is unscrewed or a cork is taken out) the CO_2 escapes in the form of bubbles. This happens because there is an imbalance between the level of CO_2 in the liquid and the air around it. Bubbles form at nucleation points: either tiny (invisible to the naked eye) pockets of air attached to the inside of the glass, or microbes of sediment on the inside of the glass with trapped air. The CO_2 in the liquid moves into these pockets, so they grow in size. As they become larger, their lower density relative to the surrounding liquid forces them to rise to the surface of the liquid. This is great as the CO_2 bubbles trap aroma molecules and bring them to the top of the liquid where they burst, launching the aroma of the drink up into your nose. When you drink a carbonated liquid the CO_2 forms bubbles inside your mouth; when it comes into contact with saliva it produces carbonic acid, a pleasant tang that adds an extra dimension to the drink.

Clarity and temperature are the key factors, so keep those in mind. If a liquid is cloudy, there will be lots of nucleation points. This means that while there may be a good amount of CO_2 dissolved into the liquid, as soon as the container is opened it will escape at a much faster rate, making it taste less fizzy. It's also so important to carbonate liquid when it's cold: water at 0°C/32°F can absorb five times more CO_2 than water at 60°C/140°F.

Below is a description of different carbonation methods. You can buy all the equipment online, or visit a homebrew store and they'll talk you through it. It can be a bit daunting at first, but when you've done it once it's a breeze.

CARBONATION RIG

This is the most efficient way to carbonate without buying a massive carbonating unit. To put one together, you need a CO_2 gas canister (you usually pay a deposit for the canister, then the gas is pretty cheap and lasts a long time), a length of ⅜inch plumbing tube and a CO_2 regulator, and carbonator cap with a ball lock, both of which are available at homebrew shops.

To set it up, attach the regulator to the CO_2 canister. Then attach the plumbing tube to the regulator with the same-sized 'John Guest fitting'. This then connects to the carbonator disconnect, and you're ready to go. You can adjust the pressure of the system with the regulator. We recommend starting at 30psi and working up until you get your desired level of carbonation.

To carbonate a liquid, fill a soda bottle two-thirds full with chilled liquid. Old, plastic fizzy drink bottles are fine. We use 1.5 or 2 litre bottles at the bar for batching. Squeeze any remaining air out of the bottle and attach the ball lock carbonator cap. Click the carbonator cap onto the rig and open the gas up. The bottle will quickly expand with CO_2 until it is under pressure. Disconnect the cap and screw the top on. Give the plastic bottle a good shake and place in the fridge for 30 minutes. Grab the bottle and in the fridge for 30 minutes. Grab the bottle and check if it is still under pressure by squeezing it. There should not be much movement. If there is, reattach it to the carbonation rig and repeat the process. If there isn't, give it another shake and allow to settle in the fridge for another 30 minutes. Open carefully, and you will have a perfectly carbonated beverage.

SODASTREAM

This is a more compact way to carbonate than a rig. However, the results are less effective and can be more expensive in the long run, as gas cartridges are costly.

SODA SIPHON/CREAM WHIPPER

These are great for charging batched cocktails (like the Cold Brew Martini, p88) or for whipping up cream instantly. They are a little simpler to set up than a carbonating rig, but the ongoing costs are higher, as you have to buy individual canisters for every use. But they are pretty easy to get hold of online, or in any decent cook shop.

The process is easy: fill the siphon with cold liquid and screw the lid on. Screw the canister into the siphon using the canister holder, wait until you hear fizzing. Shake the siphon and place the whole thing in the fridge to settle.

There are two main types of canister – carbon dioxide (CO_2) or nitrous oxide (NO_2). CO_2 will carbonate a liquid, making it like cola, say, or champagne. NO_2 will have a similar effect but with a much tighter bubble structure, so will end up with something more akin to Guinness.

Once the fizzy liquid has settled – about half an hour – pour out the liquid according to the type of canister you're using. With CO_2, expel the gas first by gently squeezing the release valve with the siphon the right way up over the sink (trust us on this one). Once all the the gas is gone, unscrew the lid and you will have a fizzy liquid. Do this just before you serve. If you have uncarbonated liquid left over, you can repeat the process. If you're using NO_2, to pour you should invert the siphon and squeeze the nozzle to release the liquid directly into a glass. Again, do this gently or you will end up with a face full of bubbles. This won't need to be recharged between serves.

MAKING 2:1 SUGAR SYRUP

One of the most-used ingredients in cocktail making is sugar syrup, sometimes called simple syrup. Weigh out two parts sugar to one part water (i.e. 500g/20oz sugar to 250g/10oz water) and combine in a bowl. Stir it sporadically over 15 minutes or so to dissolve it. Then use a funnel to transfer it to a sterilised bottle, and seal. Once bottled it will last for up to three weeks in the fridge.

SOUS VIDE

Sous vide is a quick and effective way of infusing flavour into liquid. Temperature and time can be controlled precisely, so it's super-consistent. You can get a domestic sous vide water bath for an affordable price these days, and it will also be a useful addition to your kitchen arsenal. But the recipes in the book also gives instructions for achieving similar results without a sous vide machine.

STRAINING

Depending on the viscosity of a liquid and its solids, from thin to thick, we use three different methods of straining.

Coffee filter and funnel: put the coffee filter in a funnel and run some cold water through it to remove any lint. Then put the funnel over a jug or bottle and pour through the liquid that needs to be strained.

Cheesecloth or clean tea towel (dish towel): suspend a sieve over a jug or bowl and line it with a cheesecloth or tea towel so the whole sieve is covered. Pour the liquid into the centre and let it collect in the vessel below.

Sieve: as above, but without the cheesecloth or tea towel.

WEIGHING LIQUID

Some recipes advise adding a weight by percentage of sugar or acid to a liquid. To weigh a liquid, place a bowl on a set of scales and zero them. Pour the liquid in and note the weight. To figure out how much sugar or acid to add, multiply the weight of the liquid by the percentage advised in the recipe converted into a decimal. For example, if the recipe says to add 50% sugar, multiply the weight of the liquid by 0.5 and add that weight in sugar.

We work with percentages this way because with fermenting, infusing and fat-washing you will get slight variations in the yield through absorption or evaporation, so it's can be hard to give precise volumes.

UK/USA MEASURES

We created these recipes using the metric bar measurements we're most familiar with. But we want our North American friends to enjoy them too, so to simplify conversions we rounded everything up to the bar measurements they're most familiar with, namely ounces. You'll end up with slightly more liquid to drink each time, but the ratios and therefore deliciousness will be the same!

SPRING

RHUBARB
& GRAPE

---

*Some things are worth waiting for, and the fermented rhubarb
cordial in this recipe is most definitely one of them. It makes
good use of fantastic fresh produce, and once you've stabilised the
fermented rhubarb with sugar and citric acid, it'll last for a few
months in the fridge. Meaning you can enjoy that flavour for much
longer than just the season.*

Fermented rhubarb cordial

- 300g/12oz rhubarb stalks
- 3g/¾ tsp White Labs dried champagne yeast (or another
  wine yeast)
- 1.5 litre/60oz water
- Caster (superfine) sugar
- Citric acid powder (see Eko Mail introduction, p44)

- Kilner jar or similar airtight, non-reactive container, at least
  2 litre/80oz
- Cheesecloth or clean tea towel (dish towel)
- Elastic band
- Funnel
- Coffee filter
- Jug, at least 2 litre/80oz jug

To bottle

- 350ml/14oz El Gobernador pisco
- 150ml/6oz fermented rhubarb cordial

- Sterilised bottle, at least 500ml/20oz

To serve

- Soda water
- Long strips of rhubarb stalk, removed with a peeler, to garnish

TO MAKE THE RHUBARB CORDIAL *1.* Chop the rhubarb into small pieces about 1cm/½inch in length. *2.* Put in the Kilner jar with the yeast, then pour in the water and stir. *3.* Cover with cheesecloth and secure with an elastic band, close the lid. *4.* Store in a dark place. Leave for 5–7 days to ferment, tasting daily after 2 days. You'll know when it is ready when it tastes like complex, acidic rhubarb juice. The longer you leave it the stronger the acid levels will become, until the liquid turns and tastes 'off'. Before any vinegar flavours become too pronounced, strain through the coffee filter into the jug (see p12) that is on some digital scales. *5.* Once strained, weigh the liquid (see p12). To avoid confusion, work out how much sugar and acid you will need for the next step before adding anything. *6.* Add 150% of the strained weight in sugar. *7.* Add 2.5% of the strained weight in citric acid. *8.* Stir until all the sugar has dissolved. This will take a little while so feel free to stir, walk away, come back and stir some more.

BOTTLE Pour the pisco and fermented rhubarb cordial into the bottle. Store in the fridge. It will keep for 2 months.

GLASS SERVE *1.* Slide a strip of rhubarb stalk around the inside of each glass. *2.* Fill with ice. *3.* Pour a large measure of cocktail in and top with soda.

SPRING

PEACH BELLINI

This was a drink that came to fruition in a similar way to the Rhubarb & Grape (see p16). We were fermenting some peaches, and made an amazing juice that had so much depth to it that we wanted to make it the main flavour of a drink. What better way than to use it in a version of the classic Bellini?

Peach cordial

- 200g/8oz Saturn peaches (flat ones, aka doughnut peaches)
- 3g/¾ tsp White Labs dried saison yeast (or another saison yeast)
- 1 litre/40oz water
- Caster (superfine) sugar
- Malic acid (see Eko Mail introduction, p44)

- Kilner jar or similar airtight, non-reactive container, at least 1.5 litre/60oz
- Cheesecloth or clean tea towel (dish towel)
- Elastic band
- Funnel
- Coffee filter
- Jug, at least 1 litre/40oz
- Sterilised bottle, at least 1 litre/40oz

To serve

- 200ml/8oz peach cordial
- 500ml/20oz good-quality prosecco
- Bay leaves, or another aromatic herb such as sage or thyme, to garnish
- Jug, at least 1 litre/40oz

TO MAKE THE PEACH CORDIAL

1. Chop the peaches into quarters and add to the Kilner jar with their stones and the yeast, then add the water and give it a stir. *2.* Cover with cheesecloth or a clean tea towel and an elastic band. Leave it in a warm dry place for 5–7 days to ferment. *3.* At first, taste every day, as peaches have a tendency to turn quite quickly. Toward the end, taste it twice a day. You're looking for notes of vinegar and a reduction in sweetness – but if you detect any 'off' flavours, it's time to stop. *4.* When you have a delicious, complex and floral peach juice, strain it through the coffee filter into the jug (see p12) that is on some digital scales. *5.* Weigh the strained juice, then add 70% of the strained weight in caster sugar (see p12). *6.* Stir until the sugar dissolves. Then add malic acid to taste, but in small amounts, working up, as the cordial is quite delicate. *7.* When you are happy with the balance of sugar and acidity, pour into the bottle and seal. Store in the fridge. It will keep for 1 month.

JUG SERVE *1.* Fill the jug with ice then add the peach cordial and top with the prosecco. *2.* Stir gently to mix. *3.* Pour the mixture into ice-filled wine glasses. *4.* Garnish with a bay leaf, or another aromatic herb.

TIP A splash of the cordial is great over thick and creamy vanilla cheesecake.

SENCHA COLLINS

The Tom Collins (gin, lemon, sugar and soda) is one of the real classics, simple but so refreshing. Our favourite twist is to make it with a sencha tea syrup, which adds an amazing green grass note, as well as an almost creamy texture. It's great in the early afternoon with a picnic.

Sencha syrup

– 400ml/16oz water
– 4.5g/2 tsp sencha tea leaves
– 400g/16oz caster (superfine) sugar

– Funnel
– Coffee filter
– Jug or bowl, at least 500ml/20oz
– Sterilised bottle, at least 500ml/20oz

To batch

– 500ml/20oz London dry gin
– 250ml/10oz fresh, strained lemon juice
– 150ml/6oz sencha syrup
– Jug, at least 2 litre/80oz

To serve

– Soda water

25

TO MAKE THE SENCHA SYRUP *1.* Heat up the water in a pan or kettle until you start to see the first few bubbles forming, indicating it is getting close to boiling, then take it off the heat. (You don't want it to boil vigorously, or for a long period of time, as it will reduce the oxygen content in the water and the tea won't taste as vibrant and complex as it should.) *2.* Add the sencha tea leaves and the hot water to a bowl or teapot. Let it infuse for 10 minutes. *3.* Pour the sencha tea through the filter into the jug to strain off the leaves (see p12). *4.* Add the sugar to the tea, stirring until it has completely dissolved. *5.* Bottle the syrup, leave to cool, then seal. You can store in the fridge. It will keep for up to 2 months.

BATCH *1.* Add the gin, lemon juice and sencha syrup to the jug and stir to combine. *2.* If you're prepping ahead, stick the jug in the refrigerator to let it cool down – you can add soda at the last second.

JUG SERVE *1.* When you're ready to serve, add loads of ice and some soda water to the jug. *2.* Then pour the cocktail into some rocks glasses or small tumblers.

TIPS Because green tea is so versatile this drink will be wonderful with almost any white spirit instead of gin, from vodka to pisco.

Also, experimenting with different mixers instead of soda water can work a treat. Ginger ale teams up particularly well with the sencha.

SOUTHERN
BELLE PUNCH

This is your new go-to cocktail for a large party and can be prepared way in advance and stored in the fridge. With a bowl of this in the middle of the table, you'll find that when it's your turn to get a drink, it will probably be gone! (So we strongly recommend making twice as much.)

The best punches are all about balance – here it's between the rich bourbon whiskey, sharp citrus and perfumed Earl Grey tea.

To batch

– 500ml/20oz bourbon whiskey
– 150ml/6oz fresh, strained lemon juice
– 150ml/6oz 2:1 sugar syrup (see p11)
– 20ml/¾oz maraschino liqueur
– 10ml/2 tsp Angostura bitters
– 400ml/16oz strong Earl Grey tea, chilled
– 400ml/16oz chilled water

– A few Tupperware-type tubs, to make large ice cubes
– Large punch bowl or similar, able to hold 3 litres/120oz

To serve

– Plenty of punch cups or small glasses
– A selection of edible flowers, seasonal fruit, citrus fruits, berries or mint sprigs, to garnish

BATCH *1.* The day before you want to serve this, fill a few plastic Tupperware-type tubs with water and put in the freezer, to create large blocks of ice for the punch. *2.* A few hours before you want to serve, simply add all the ingredients to your chosen punch bowl and stick it in the fridge to get it nice and cold. It will keep for 24 hours.

BOWL SERVE *1.* Pull the bowl out of the fridge, and get the large ice blocks out of the freezer and place in the bowl. *2.* Get extravagant with the garnishes: as it is a centrepiece, you can go overboard with edible flowers, seasonal fruit and mint sprigs. If you can't get hold of fancy garnishes, citrus wheels look great bobbing just under the surface along with mint sprigs and berries. *3.* Just leave a ladle in the bowl and let your guests help themselves.

TIPS This recipe, like most punches, will still be delicious with different spirits. So, feel free to swap the bourbon for gin, rum, cognac, vodka or whatever you prefer. The same goes for the liqueur. Maraschino is a cherry liqueur, but can be changed for a liqueur of your choice. You can also play around with the tea element. Earl Grey is used here as it has floral notes that work well with maraschino. But try rum with Assam tea and peach liqueur, or Scotch, lapsang souchong and apricot, or even tequila, green tea and pear liqueur.

PALM MILK
PUNCH

Milk punch is, as the name suggests, a milk-based drink with spirits (usually brandy and rum) as well as gentle spices. Our amped-up version includes palm wine, made from the sap of palm trees, and rhum agricole, a cane-sugar rum from the French Caribbean. It's packed with spices and is great to sip before sitting down for some food.

To bottle

- 200ml/8oz light rum
- 200ml/8oz palm wine
- 100ml/4oz rhum agricole
- 12g/2 tbsp lemon peel
- 10g/1¼ tbsp chopped tiger nut
- 4 cloves
- 1 seed of grain of selim (see 'Wine' introduction, p114)
- 20g/¾oz acacia honey
- 0.5g/¼ tsp whole allspice
- 100ml/4oz fresh, strained lemon juice
- 200ml/8oz whole milk
- Caster (superfine) sugar

- Cooking thermometer
- Funnel
- Coffee filter
- 2 jugs, at least 1 litre/40oz
- Sterilised bottle, at least 1 litre/40oz

To serve

- Edible flowers, to garnish

BOTTLE *1.* This method may have many steps to it, but it is fairly straightforward. Put the ingredients into a saucepan with the exception of the lemon juice, milk and sugar: they come in later. *2.* Using the thermometer, heat the liquid to between 50°C/122°F and 55°C/131°F and cook for 30 minutes. You will need to be vigilant as you do not want to burn off any of the alcohol, so make sure the temperature does not rise to 60°C/140°F. Alternatively, cook sous vide for 30 minutes at 52.5°C/126.5°F (see p12). *3.* After 30 minutes strain the liquid through a coffee filter into one of the jugs and set aside (see p12). *4.* Add the lemon juice to the cooked alcohol in the jug. *5.* Heat the milk in a saucepan on a medium heat until just before boiling point. A good time to remove it from the heat is when the liquid first starts to roll. Add it immediately to the alcohol and lemon mix. *6.* You should start to see large, cloud-like curds forming straight away. *7.* Cover with cling film (plastic wrap) and put in the fridge for 2 hours. *8.* After 2 hours set up the funnel and a coffee filter over the other jug and strain the mixture through. This step can take a long time, so we recommend setting it up in the fridge and leaving it overnight. *9.* Sometimes the first strain does not produce the crystal-clear liquid you want. If this is the case, just pass the strained liquid through the same coffee filter you used the first time, and it will be clear when you come back to it. *10.* Once the straining is finished weigh the liquid and add 10% of that weight in sugar (see p12). *11.* Stir to dissolve the sugar – it shouldn't take long. *12.* Transfer to the bottle, seal and store in the fridge. It will keep for 6 months.

GLASS SERVE *1.* Add ice to rocks glasses and fill them with the palm milk punch. *2.* Garnish with some edible flowers, which will contrast with the opaqueness of the liquid and look stunning.

TIPS Swapping out the lemon for lime, both the peel and fresh juice, will give an extra-tropical feel to this drink.

Also, you can experiment with different spices: the likes of cinnamon, star anise, cloves and nutmeg will be ideal. Remember to start with small amounts and work your way up.

RANGOON
ICE TEA

On a holiday in Myanmar, Max was taken aback by the quality of the food, particularly a local dish of pickled tea salad with fried almonds and lime – 'lahpet thoke'. The completeness of the flavour was astounding: freshness, acidity, tannin and texture. It's often served to share at parties, and we wanted to translate that to a drink. So what better way to do it than as a punch, that ultimate bowl-based sharing drink. You can garnish it elaborately, so make it a centrepiece – it's perfect for an afternoon gathering.

If you want to read more about the fascinating history of punch (well, we think it's fascinating!), get yourself David Wondrich's book 'Punch: the Delights (and Dangers) of the Flowing Bowl'. Experts like him agree that the main challenges with making punch are avoiding over-dilution and getting the balance of all the ingredients right, but this recipe should nail it.

To batch

– 4g/1½ tsp dried almond flowers (best from the
  Rare Tea Company)
– 5g/2 tsp Assam or other black tea leaves
– 200g/8oz orange flower honey
– 300ml/12oz London dry gin – Beefeater is ideal,
  as the almond used in its distillation will shine through
– 75ml/3oz fresh, strained lemon juice
– 75ml/3oz fresh, strained lime juice
– 5ml/1 tsp Angostura bitters

– Coffee filters
– Funnel
– Jug or container, at least 1 litre/40oz

To serve

– A punch bowl, or other big bowl you'd be happy to display at a party
– Dainty glasses to ladle the punch into
– 300ml/12oz soda water
– Aromatic edible flowers, to garnish
– Citrus peel – orange, lemon, lime or grapefruit – to garnish

BATCH 1. First off, brew the teas separately. In a saucepan, heat 400ml/16oz of water to just off boiling temperature, around 80°C/176°F. **2.** Pour it over the dried almond flowers in a jug or teapot, and leave to infuse for 15 minutes. **3.** Strain through a coffee filter into the jug (see p12). You can save the flowers and brew them again for a relaxing caffeine-free tea. **4.** Heat 200ml/8oz of water to just off boiling temperature, again. **5.** Brew the black tea in a jug or teapot, for 8 minutes this time. **6.** Strain through a coffee filter into the almond tea in the jug. **7.** Let the tea mix cool, and then stir in the rest of the ingredients. **8.** Cover and chill in the fridge. It will keep for 24 hours.

BOWL SERVE 1. When you're ready to serve, fill a nice punch bowl with ice, and pour the mixture in. **2.** Top with the soda water and gently mix. **3.** Garnish with the edible flowers and some citrus peel, and ladle into dainty glasses.

SPRING

TEQUILA
& MEAD

Mead is a traditional fermented honey 'wine', said to be the oldest alcoholic drink in the world. Technically this version isn't mead because it uses agave instead of honey, but it has a similar mouthfeel and balance. When Max was in Mexico, he tried some fermented agave juice ('pulque'). While he found it interesting, he wasn't madly into it. But it made him think about fermenting agave syrup, which is available in the UK, and what we could then do with it. This is a great way to get into simple fermentation. Get a bottle chilled and take it to a picnic.

Agave mead
– 200ml/8oz high-quality agave syrup
– 800ml/32oz water
– 3g/¾ tsp brewer's yeast
– 5g/1¾ tsp citric acid powder (see Eko Mail introduction, p44)
– Funnel
– Jug or container, at least 1.5 litre/60oz
– 5 x 200ml/8oz plastic bottles (or 3 x 330ml/13oz)

To serve
– 40ml/1½oz blanco tequila per serve – the Ocho brand is the one for us
– Agave mead
– Lime wedges, to garnish

TO MAKE THE AGAVE MEAD

1. Put the ingredients into the jug and mix together until everything has dissolved. *2.* Split between the plastic bottles (plastic is safer for fermenting), seal and keep in a cool place, but not in the fridge. Leave for 5 days or so. If you're worried about exploding bottles, use a large plastic tub with a lid instead. *3.* If the bottles look out of shape, the pressure may be building too much. Release it by unscrewing the cap very slowly, then putting the cap back on. *4.* Taste daily after 2 days. When ready it will have a slight note of alcohol, the yeast aroma will have faded and it will have lost some sweetness. There should be a creamy mouthfeel and good fizz. *5.* After 5 or so days, release the pressure again, and refrigerate. Once refrigerated they will last for at least 1 month.

GLASS SERVE *1.* Fill highball glasses with ice and pour the tequila into each. *2.* Top with agave mead and garnish with a lime wedge.

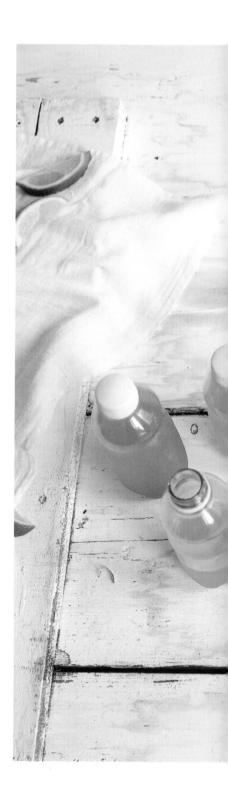

EKO MAIL

We came up with this twist on the classic Air Mail (rum, lime, honey and champagne) for Ikoyi, an incredible West African restaurant in London that belongs to a friend of ours.

It uses a mix of citric and malic acid – these occur naturally within fruits such as lemons and apples. The powder form is the concentrate, and you can buy it in specialist food shops or online. It adds acidity, like citrus, and slows down spoiling, but doesn't have a dominating flavour.

Verjus is an acidic juice made from pressing unripe grapes. It has similar characteristics to vinegar, with less raw acidity. It's a great alternative to lemon or lime, and is stocked by specialist food shops.

Citric and malic mix

- 4g/heaped tsp citric acid powder
- 2g/½ tsp malic acid powder
- 94g/3¾oz water, weighed using digital scales
- Jug or bowl, at least 100ml/4oz
- Sterilised bottle, at least 100ml/4oz

To bottle

- 120ml/4¾oz Havana Club 3-year-old rum
- 25ml/1oz Minus 8 Red Verjus
- 25ml/1oz acacia honey
- 25ml/1oz 2:1 sugar syrup (see p11)
- 35ml/1½oz citric and malic mix
- 170ml//6¾oz dry white wine
- 1ml/dash orange flower water
- 340ml/13½oz chilled water

- Jug or bowl, at least 750ml/30oz
- Preferred carbonation method (SodaStream, siphon or carbonation rig, see p9)
- Funnel
- Sterilised bottle, at least 750ml/30oz

TO MAKE THE CITRIC AND MALIC MIX *1.* Add the citric acid powder, malic acid powder and the water to the jug. *2.* Stir until all the powder has dissolved. *3.* Store in the small bottle in the fridge, sealed, and it will keep almost indefinitely.

BOTTLE *1.* Put all the ingredients into the jug and stir to combine everything. *2.* Place in the fridge until it gets nice and cold. *3.* Once chilled, carbonate using your preferred method (see p9). *4.* Using the funnel, carefully transfer to the bottle and seal. Store in the fridge. It will keep for 1 week.

CITRUS
CORDIALS

---

*More and more bartenders are beginning to address the issue of
sustainability. For us, it has become an important part of our
day-to-day operations. We go through a lot of lemon juice in the
bar and are often left with piles of husks. So we use them to make
lemon water to drink, or we dry them out to infuse into alcohol.
And another way to use them is to make a cordial – this has a
decent shelf life, so you don't have to use it straight away. Use the
cordial in a cocktail (like the Lemon & Cardamom Gimlet, p72),
or in a non-alcoholic mixed drink.*

To bottle

- Leftover citrus husks (lemon, lime, orange or grapefruit etc.),
  at least 200g/8oz
- The same weight in caster (superfine) sugar
- The same weight in water
- Citric acid powder, optional (see Eko Mail introduction, p44)
- Funnel
- Coffee filter
- Sterilised bottle, at least 1 litre/40oz

To serve

- Soda water
- A white spirit such as vodka, unaged tequila or light rum –
  nothing too oaky (optional)

TO BOTTLE *1.* Put the spent citrus husks in a bowl, pour the sugar over the husks. You can make a single-citrus cordial, or mix them all together for a combination of citrus flavours. *2.* Muddle the sugar into the citrus to release the oils. Cover and leave it in a cool place, overnight if possible or at least for a few hours. *3.* Add the water and stir until the sugar is dissolved, then rest for an hour or so. *4.* Strain off the liquid through a coffee filter into another jug (see p12). (For extra eco points, compost the leftover husks.) *5.* Taste the cordial for acidity – if you feel you need to add a little citric acid to taste, then do, but this isn't essential. Some people like a tangy cordial. *6.* If you've added citric acid, stir to dissolve. *7.* Transfer to the bottle and seal. Store in a cool place. It will keep for 1 month.

GLASS SERVE *1.* For a refreshing non-alcoholic drink, pour 40ml/1½oz citrus cordial over ice in a highball. *2.* Top with soda water.

1. To give it an alcoholic spike, pour 50ml/2oz spirit of your choice (gin or vodka are particularly good) over ice in a highball. *2.* Add 25ml/1oz cordial and top with soda water.

TIP If you have some spare herbs that need using up, or you want to add a herbal dimension to the cordial, you can add these when you are muddling the sugar with the citrus. Herbs such as basil or parsley work really nicely. You'll need about 5% of the weight of the husks in herbs (see p12) – this should add a good amount of flavour.

SUMMER

JASMINE

HYACINTHE LESCOET, LES GRANDS VERRES, PARIS, FRANCE

This cocktail recipe was donated by our pal Hyacinthe, a larger-than-life Frenchman with a full beard and broad shoulders, that belie his soft accent, knowledge and ability to create delicious, delicate drinks.

There are many varieties of jasmine: white jasmine or 'poet's jasmine' (jasminum officinale) usually blooms any time from spring through to autumn. It grows wild, so you can forage for it once you learn to identify the plant – this is especially appealing, as buying jasmine flowers can be prohibitively expensive.

This cocktail is a lighter way to enjoy cognac, as it shows off its floral, aromatic quality, rather than its rich, woody notes. It's a beautiful drink to serve in a simple carafe, and drink slowly through the course of an evening, together with a good friend.

SUMMER

Jasmine cordial

- 140ml/5½oz water
- 6g/⅓oz fresh jasmine
- 70g/2¾oz caster (superfine) sugar
- 2.5g/½ tsp citric acid powder (see Eko Mail introduction, p44)
- Digital cooking thermometer
- Funnel
- Small clean, empty bottle, at least 175ml/7oz

To bottle

(equal parts, depending on how much cordial you end up with)
- 175ml/7oz water
- 175ml/7oz cognac
- 175ml/7oz jasmine cordial
- 175ml/7oz dry vermouth (we like Dolin Vermouth de
  Chambéry Dry for this)

- Jug, at least 1 litre/40oz
- Sterilised bottle, at least 700ml/28oz

To serve

- Jasmine flowers, to garnish

TO MAKE THE JASMINE CORDIAL *1.* In a saucepan, gently heat the water to 60°C/140°F. *2.* Add the jasmine, take off the heat and leave to infuse for 30 minutes. *3.* Scoop out the jasmine, or strain through a sieve into a jug or bowl. *4.* Add the sugar and citric acid, then stir to dissolve. This should produce approximately 175ml/7oz of cordial. *5.* Transfer to the bottle, seal and store in the fridge. It will keep for 1 month.

BOTTLE *1.* Put all the ingredients into the jug and stir to combine. *2.* Transfer to the bottle and seal. It can be stored in the fridge or freezer for up to 1 month.

GLASS SERVE *1.* Just pour a measure straight from the chilled bottle into a glass. *2.* If you have some jasmine flowers to hand, use one to garnish.

TARRAGON & GRAPEFRUIT COLLINS

The bittersweet, mildly aniseed flavour of tarragon teams up well with the acidity from the pink grapefruit in this drink, and it's a perfect refresher to sip on a warm weekend afternoon in the park. It's also more than a match for spicy food.

This recipe should make enough for about 10 people.

Tarragon syrup

- 150ml/6oz 2:1 sugar syrup (see p11)
- 75g/3oz fresh tarragon
- Tupperware-type or other lidded container, large enough to hold the 2:1 sugar syrup and tarragon
- Sterilised bottle, at least 150ml/6oz

To batch

- 500ml/20oz gin
- 150ml/6oz fresh, strained grapefruit juice
- 100ml/4oz fresh, strained lemon juice
- 150ml/6oz tarragon syrup
- Jug, at least 2 litre/80oz

To serve

- Soda water
- Tarragon stems or slices of grapefruit, to garnish

TO MAKE THE TARRAGON SYRUP

1. Combine the sugar syrup and tarragon in the container, seal and leave to infuse overnight, or for a few hours at least, in the fridge. *2.* Strain through a sieve (see p12). *3.* Transfer to the bottle and seal. It will keep for quite a while in the fridge: 2 months is a good guideline.

BATCH *1.* A couple of hours before you want to serve, add all the ingredients to the jug and put in the fridge.

JUG SERVE *1.* Fill the jug with ice and top with soda water, giving it a quick stir to combine everything. *2.* Fill some tall glasses with ice and pour from the jug. *3.* To garnish, take some tarragon stems and give them a slap to release their aroma, then slide one down the side of each glass. If you only bought enough tarragon to make the syrup, a nice slice of grapefruit is equally as pretty.

TIP The combination of the aniseed notes from the tarragon and fresh citrus means this drink can be made with a couple of different spirits. Vodka amplifies the herb and grapefruit, while blanco tequila's tangy flavour is good too.

FENNEL & ELDERFLOWER FIZZ

*This is perfect for a picnic and really easy to prep the day before.
The savoury note from the fennel means this pairs well with light
food. Along with the prosecco and a few fronds of fennel
to garnish, it makes for a very sophisticated summer tipple.*

Elderflower and fennel cordial

– 200g/8oz bulb fennel
– 500ml/20oz elderflower cordial – Belvoir is really good
– Plastic tub or bowl, at least 750ml/30oz
– Funnel
– Coffee filter

To serve

– 25ml/1oz elderflower and fennel cordial per serve
– 100ml/4oz prosecco per serving
– Fennel slices and fennel leaves, to garnish

TO MAKE THE ELDERFLOWER AND FENNEL CORDIAL *1.* Slice the fennel
very thinly – if you have a mandoline use that, otherwise use a sharp knife and go as
fine as you can. Keep some of the sliced fennel for garnishing, plus the leaves if they're
there. *2.* Place it in the tub, pour the elderflower cordial over, cover with a lid or cling
film (plastic wrap) and leave in the fridge for 24 hours. Keep the empty cordial bottle:
you will need it later. Alternatively, cook the fennel and cordial sous vide for
30 minutes at 52°C/126°F, then allow to cool (see p12). *3.* Strain through a coffee filter
into the empty cordial bottle (see p12). It will keep in the fridge for up to 1 week.

GLASS SERVE *1.* If you're taking this to a picnic, fill a cool box with ice and put in the prosecco and the cordial. *2.* If you've saved leaves from the fennel, wrap them in damp kitchen (paper) towel with the fennel slices to keep them fresh, and place them on the ice. *3.* To serve, put some ice cubes in each wine glass and add the cordial. Top with prosecco and stir. *4.* Add the fennel leaves and slices to garnish.

FRENCH 75

*Although this is quite a detour from the classic French 75
formulation (gin, lemon, sugar, champagne), it's a great cocktail
for a celebration or pre-dinner aperitif; it takes a little patience
but is well worth it. We have regular customers who never drink
anything else.*

To bottle
- 110ml/4¼oz Star of Bombay gin
- 180ml/7¼oz minerally, dry white wine
- 50ml/2oz Minus 8 Maple Brix Verjus (see Eko Mail
  introduction, p44)
- 25ml/1oz Minus 8 Red Verjus
- 45ml/1¾oz 2:1 sugar syrup (see p11)
- 1ml/dash orange flower water
- 345ml/13¾oz chilled water
- 30ml/1¼oz fresh, unstrained lemon juice

- 2 jugs, at least 1 litre/40oz
- Funnel
- Coffee filter
- Preferred carbonating method (SodaStream, soda siphon/
  cream whipper or carbonation rig, see p9)
- Sterilised bottle, at least 1 litre/40oz

BOTTLE *1.* Combine all the ingredients in one of the jugs, adding the lemon juice last.
Don't stir! ***2.*** Place in the fridge for around 30 minutes. ***3.*** When you go back to the
mix you'll start to notice a cloud-like formation floating to the top. This means it's
ready to strain; pour through the coffee filter and collect the liquid in the other jug
(see p12). ***4.*** Put it in the fridge to get it cold. ***5.*** Once cold, carbonate using whichever
method suits you (see p9). ***6.*** Pour it carefully (to keep the fizz) into the bottle and seal.
Store in the fridge. It will keep for 1 week.

GLASS SERVE *1.* Pour into a flute, or over ice in a wine glass if you fancy.

SUMMER

AMERICANO VERGANO

This drink came about when our wine supplier gave us a taste of a bitter amaro from northern Italy called Vergano Americano. We enjoyed it so much that we had it in a drink on the menu the next day. This is a low-alcohol, easy-drinking twist on the Americano (Campari, sweet vermouth and soda): we added citrus to increase the bitterness and freshness. It's great for a barbecue, as you can put it together in the afternoon ready to go in the evening.

To batch

– 500ml/20oz Vergano Americano (see tip below)
– 250ml/10oz fresh, strained pink grapefruit juice
– 150ml/6oz fresh, strained lemon juice
– 50ml/2oz 2:1 sugar syrup (see p11)

– Jug, 2 litre/80oz

To serve

– Soda water
– Pink grapefruit or orange wedges, to garnish
– Mint leaves, to garnish (optional)

BATCH *1.* Add the ingredients straight into the jug, cover and put in the fridge. It will keep for 48 hours.

JUG SERVE *1.* When you're ready to go, add ice to the jug with a few slices of grapefruit, and mint leaves if you have some. *2.* Fill glasses with ice, add some of the mix and top with soda water.

TIP If you can't get hold of Americano Vergano, use 300ml/12oz decent dry white wine and 200ml/8oz Campari instead.

FORAGED
MARTINI

*This is a gentler (and more exciting) version of the Martini,
but it doesn't transform it too dramatically. It's a great example
of how subtle changes can affect a classic drink. Plus, you can
bottle-age it. A good way to do this is to make two bottles: one
to age and one to drink. If you store one in a cool, dark place
for anything over 6 months, you will begin to taste changes in
the flavour profile. Think of it like wine – the small amount
of oxygen in the bottle will slowly interact with the different
ingredients until they start to combine and produce new aroma
compounds, which will increase the complexity and depth.*

Nettle cordial

- 100g/4oz washed nettle leaves
- 500ml/20oz water
- 75g/3oz caster (superfine) sugar
- 20g/¾oz citric acid powder (see Eko Mail introduction, p44)
- Kilner jar or similar airtight, non-reactive container, at least
  1 litre/40oz

To bottle

- 375ml/15oz London dry gin
- 125ml/5oz dry vermouth
- 40ml/1½oz nettle cordial
- 175ml/7oz chilled water

- Jug, at least 1 litre/40oz
- Sterilised bottle, at least 700ml/28oz

To serve

- Gysophila, or other pretty flower, to garnish
- Lemon zests, to garnish

TO MAKE THE NETTLE CORDIAL

1. Add the nettle leaves to the Kilner jar.
2. In a pan, bring the water to just below
boiling. *3.* Pour it over the nettle leaves
in the jar. Seal the lid. *4.* Leave overnight
to infuse. *5.* The next day, strain the
leaves from the liquid using a sieve
(see p12) and then return the liquid to
the jar. *6.* Add the sugar and citric acid.
Stir until dissolved. Store in the fridge.
It will keep for 1 month.

BOTTLE *1.* Add the gin, vermouth
and nettle cordial to the jug. *2.* Add
the chilled water and stir to combine
everything. *3.* Pour the mix into the bottle
and seal. *4.* Store in the freezer. It will
keep for 1 year.

GLASS SERVE *1.* When you are ready
to serve, pour directly into chilled Martini
glasses, to the brim. *2.* Garnish with
flowers (at the edge of the glass). *3.* Then
twist the lemon zest over the glass to
release the oils.

TIPS You can use the nettle cordial with
soda to make a really refreshing non-
alcoholic drink. Just add 25ml/1oz of
cordial to a tall glass with ice and top
with soda.

If nettle cordial is not for you, swap
it for another fresh cordial such as
elderflower or dandelion, which will
also work well in a Martini.

LEMON & CARDAMOM GIMLET

This involves an ancient method of flavour extraction known as an oleo saccharum, in which sugar pulls oils from citrus. It was used a lot in 19th-century cocktail making. Along with perfumed cardamom, it creates a delicate and easy-drinking gimlet (classically, sweetened lime juice and gin) perfect for a bright evening.

Lemon and cardamom cordial

- 10 lemons
- 5 cardamom pods
- 400g/16oz caster (superfine) sugar

- Wide, shallow bowl
- Cheesecloth or clean tea towel (dish towel)
- Jug, at least 1 litre/40oz
- Sterilised bottle, at least 1 litre/40oz

To bottle

- 350ml/14oz gin
- 200ml/8oz lemon and cardamom cordial
- 200ml/8oz water

- Sterilised bottle, at least 750ml/30oz

TO MAKE THE LEMON AND CARDAMOM CORDIAL *1.* Zest the lemons into the bowl with a fine grater, reserving the fruits. *2.* Split the cardamom pods to remove the seeds, then crush them with a pestle and mortar and add to the bowl. *3.* Pour over the sugar and muddle together for 5–10 minutes to combine. You will see the sugar turning yellowish. *4.* Leave it, covered, for an hour. *5.* When infused, juice the lemons then add the juice to the mixture and stir until dissolved. *6.* Strain this through the cheesecloth into the jug, then transfer to the bottle and seal. Store in the fridge for up to 6 weeks.

BOTTLE *1.* Combine the gin, cordial and water in the bottle, seal and store in the freezer. It keeps for 6 months.

GLASS SERVE *1.* Pour to the brim of a chilled cocktail glass.

TIP The cordial is delicious with still or sparkling water. Just mix one part cordial to three parts water over ice in a tall glass.

PEAR
& PASTIS

The distinctive aniseed notes in this drink may divide opinion, but it's a lovely, tall, refreshing number to kick back with in the early evening, and those who enjoy the grown-up flavour of pastis will absolutely adore it.

To bottle

- 350ml/14oz vodka
- 100ml/4oz pear liqueur
- 100ml/4oz 2:1 sugar syrup (see p11)
- 20ml/¾oz pastis
- 285ml/11½oz fresh, strained lemon juice

- Jug, at least 1 litre/40oz
- Funnel
- Sterilised bottle, at least 1 litre/40oz

To serve

- Soda water
- Lemon slices, to garnish

BOTTLE *1.* This is so easy to knock up in the afternoon before an evening occasion. Mix all the liquid ingredients in the jug. *2.* Transfer to the bottle. *3.* Store in the fridge to chill. It will keep for 24 hours.

GLASS SERVE *1.* Fill some highballs with ice. *2.* Pour 75ml/3oz of the cocktail into each glass and top with soda. *3.* Give it a quick stir and garnish with a lemon slice.

TIPS If you are not a fan of pastis, this drink will work without. If pear is not your favourite flavour, another fruit liqueur can be used – peach or apricot both work well.

To add a fun bit of spice, it can also be topped with a good-quality ginger beer instead of soda water.

PANACHE

This may be the first proper drink we ever tried. Our grandparents spent half their time in the Dordogne area of southern France when we were growing up, so every summer we drove down for a month in the school holidays. Perhaps a little precocious, we often persuaded mum to let us have a shandy or two (or, as it's known there, a 'panaché', local beer with fizzy lemonade). And still to this day whenever we have a panaché, shandy or even lager tops, it takes us back to those hot days in the Midi-Pyrénées. We wanted to recreate the essence of that but with a contemporary lift.

Bergamot lemon sherbet

- 20g/³⁄₄oz grated lemon zest
- 200g/8oz caster (superfine) sugar
- 200ml/8oz fresh, strained lemon juice
- 200ml/8oz water
- 2 drops food-grade bergamot oil (optional, but worth it)

- 2 jugs or containers, at least 1 litre/40oz
- Sterilised bottle, at least 1 litre/40oz
- Cheesecloth or clean tea towel (dish towel)

To bottle

- Bergamot lemon sherbet
- Chilled bottles of light beer – pilsner or a very light pale ale

TO MAKE THE BERGAMOT LEMON SHERBET *1.* Place the lemon zest and sugar in one of the jugs and muddle them together. *2.* Add the lemon juice, water and bergamot oil, then stir. *3.* Allow to sit until the oils are infused and the sugar is dissolved, about an hour. *4.* Strain through the cheesecloth or tea towel into the other jug (see p12). Transfer to the bottle and seal. *5.* Store in the fridge. It will keep for 1 month.

BOTTLE *1.* Open a fridge-cold bottle of beer and pour away (or better, drink) a decent mouthful. *2.* Gently pour in 25ml/1oz of the sherbet and push the cap back onto the bottle. Store in the fridge. It will keep for 48 hours. To serve, crack open and drink from the bottle, or pour into a glass if you're feeling fancy.

STRAWBERRY SODA

*This is an amazing way of getting a whole summer out
of strawberry season. Once made it will sit in the fridge until
autumn. You can add extra booze if you like, but it is delicious
by itself (and ever-so-slightly alcoholic, probably less than
1% ABV). There are various options here, so read the recipe
carefully before starting.*

Strawberry ferment (for 'cordial' or 'bottle ferment')
– 200g/8oz strawberries
– 200g/8oz caster (superfine) sugar
– 2g/½ tsp dried brewer's yeast, for the 'bottle ferment'
– Kilner jar or similar airtight, non-reactive container, at least
   1 litre/40oz
– Jug, at least 1 litre/40oz
– Funnel
– Coffee filter
– Sterilised bottle, at least 1 litre/40oz or, for the 'cordial', or
   6 x plastic bottles, about 200ml/8oz each, with caps for the
   'bottle ferment'

To serve
– Soda water (optional)
– Light rum (optional)

TO MAKE THE STRAWBERRY FERMENT *1*. Halve the strawberries and add them
to the Kilner jar, stems and all. *2*. Pour the sugar on top. *3*. Cover with a cheesecloth
or tea towel and seal the lid over the cloth. Leave somewhere dark for up to 10 days.
Start tasting daily after 2 days. Over time it will develop a heavy syrup at the base. It
should be a little fizzy, and taste sweet with a rich strawberry flavour. There will be a
slight alcohol aroma off the top due to natural fermentation. Stop before any vinegary
or 'off' flavours make themselves known.

SUMMER

Now you can go down two routes: make a *cordial*, or *bottle ferment*.

CORDIAL *1*. In the jug, mix the strawberry ferment with 400ml/16oz water and stir for 10 minutes or so to dissolve any sugar. *2*. Leave to sit for an hour. *3*. Strain the liquid through a coffee filter (see p12) into the bottle and seal. *4*. Store in the fridge up to 1 month.

OR

BOTTLE FERMENT *1*. Add 1 litre/40oz water to the strawberry ferment. Stir and sit for an hour, then strain the liquid into the jug. *2*. Add the dried brewer's yeast and stir to combine. *3*. Split this between the plastic bottles, screw on the caps and leave to ferment for 3 days in a cool place. If the bottles look out of shape the pressure may be building. Release it by unscrewing slowly then putting the cap back on. *4*. After 3 days, add a small pinch of citric acid to each bottle and store in the fridge for up to 3 months.

GLASS SERVE *1*. You can serve the cordial or the bottle ferment neat, or with a measure of light rum. Add soda water for a delicious long drink.

SUMMER

CUMIN
PALOMA

We came up with this smoky version of the classic Paloma (tequila, grapefruit and soda) for International Tequila Week, which is in the middle of summer. When we get that rare glorious weekend of uninterrupted sun in the UK, this drink springs to mind. Make it in the morning and it'll be perfect for afternoon sipping in the garden while your mates take care of the barbecue.

Cumin tequila

- 450ml/18oz blanco tequila
- 1.5g/1 tsp cumin seeds
- Kilner jar or similar airtight, non-reactive container, at least 500ml/20oz
- Sterilised bottle, at least 500ml/20oz

To serve

- 350ml/14oz cumin tequila
- 250ml/10oz fresh, strained pink grapefruit juice
- 15ml/½oz tomato vinegar (alternatively, 7.5ml/¼oz red wine vinegar)
- 35ml/1½oz 2:1 sugar syrup (see p11)
- Soda water
- Pink grapefruit wedges, to garnish

TO MAKE THE CUMIN TEQUILA *1.* Measure 350ml/14oz of the tequila and pour it into the Kilner jar. *2.* Toast the cumin seeds in a non-stick frying pan on a medium heat. Keep an eye on them as you don't want to burn the seeds. Once you can smell toasted cumin, they are ready. *3.* Add the cumin to the tequila in the Kilner jar. Seal the jar shut and give it a quick shake to incorporate the seeds throughout the spirit. *4.* Leave to infuse for 3 hours. *5.* Strain the infused tequila through a sieve (see p12), transfer to the bottle. *6.* Add the remaining uninfused tequila to the bottle. *7.* Put the cap on the bottle and give a gentle shake to mix everything together. It will keep indefinitely.

BATCH *1.* Add the cumin tequila, pink grapefruit juice, tomato vinegar and sugar syrup to a carafe or jug. You can keep this in the fridge until you're ready to serve. It will keep for 24 hours.

JUG SERVE *1*. Fill the glasses with ice, add 100ml/4oz of the cocktail from the carafe, and top with soda water. *2.* Garnish with pretty wedges of pink grapefruit.

TIP In the bar we char the pink grapefruit wedges for the garnish with a blowtorch. At home you can do this by holding them in tongs over a flame on the hob. This adds an extra layer of scent and flavour.

COLD BREW
MARTINI

The Espresso Martini has become the drink of our time.
It's a punchy pre-party stiffener, or something to get you back on
track after a late night. In most recipes there's a fair amount of
sugar or liqueur to balance the bitterness from the coffee. But in
order to drop the sugar levels, we like to use cold brew coffee – it
doesn't have the same bitterness and comes with a rounder flavour.
We then dispense it from a soda siphon, which gives the drink
a velvety, Guinness-like texture. However, you can make this
without a siphon – see the tip at the end (p90).

To batch
- 700ml/28oz cold water
- 110g/4½oz ground coffee – if you have a preferred roaster,
  get some freshly ground; it's the main body of the drink, so
  make sure it's decent
- 150ml/6oz vodka (or you can use tequila or rum)
- 75g/3oz caster (superfine) sugar

- 2 jugs or containers, at least 2 litre/80oz
- Funnel
- Coffee filter
- Soda siphon/cream whipper
- NO₂ cartridge

BATCH *1.* Pour the water over the ground coffee in one of the jugs. Stir for 20 seconds to release some of the gases in the coffee (this is known as the bloom). *2.* Cover and leave overnight in a cool place, or for at least 10 hours. (Max – the morning brother – does this when he makes his brew in the morning for the cocktail later that night.) *3.* Strain the liquid through the coffee filter into the other jug (see p12). It will keep in this form (covered in the fridge) for a couple of days. *4.* Add the vodka and sugar, and stir until dissolved. *5.* Pour into the siphon and charge with the canister (see p11). Shake and put in the fridge to rest until chilled, about 2 hours.

GLASS SERVE *1.* Very gently squeeze the nozzle on the siphon to release the liquid into each glass and allow to settle. *2.* Top off to fill the glasses.

TIP If you don't have a soda siphon, you can make this with a cocktail shaker instead. Put 150ml/6oz of the mix into the shaker. Fill with ice and shake hard, then strain it into a cocktail glass.

HOWIE IN THE JUNGLE

NATHAN MCCARLEY-O'NEILL, THE NOMAD HOTEL, NYC, USA

When Nathan moved to New York City in 2015, London lost a bright talent, but his drinks at the bar in the NoMad Hotel are a fine reason to visit the second greatest city in the world. His cocktail is a superbly fresh pre-dinner drink, complex but fruity at the same time. It's straightforward and ideal to mix up in advance of a dinner party. It contains pineapple juice – it's best if you can juice it yourself (using an electric juicer), but if you're buying it make sure it isn't made from concentrate and is 100% pressed. Also, squeeze the lime just before you batch the mix.

To batch

- 100ml/4oz Cherry Heering liqueur
- 150ml/6oz strained pineapple juice
- 150ml/6oz fresh, strained lime juice
- 150ml/6oz Aperol
- 300ml/12oz Zucca (an Italian aperitif)

- Jug or container, at least 1 litre/40oz

To serve

- Soda water
- Mint sprigs, to garnish
- Colourful edible flowers, to garnish

BATCH 1. Put all the ingredients together in the jug and stir to combine. **2.** Cover and refrigerate until your guests arrive. It will keep for 24 hours, so best to make on the day.

JUG SERVE 1. When you're ready to serve, stir the mix again, then pour 2 large measures – about 100ml/4oz – into a highball over ice for each guest. **2.** Top with 50ml/2oz of soda and stir to combine. **3.** Garnish with a mint sprig for some fresh aroma, and some colourful flowers for wow factor.

SUMMER

A LIFE LESS ORDINARY

ALEX PROUDFOOT, MANCHESTER, UK

*Alex is a great friend of ours, and he really understands how
flavour works. He has an amazing ability to make drinks that
you simply have to have more than one of: the recipe below is
a perfect example. Noel and Alex worked together in Manchester
at Crazy Pedro's Part-Time Pizza Parlour. It was a bar that
specialised in tequila and its more rustic Mexican cousin mezcal,
so it's no surprise that Alex's drink has a mezcal base. It's a
great welcome drink for guests if you're having a barbecue or
garden party.*

This recipe serves five.

Melon syrup

- 125g/5oz fresh honeydew melon flesh, peeled
- 250ml/10oz 2:1 sugar syrup (see p11)

- Plastic container with a lid, or similar, at least 500ml/20oz
- Funnel
- Coffee filter
- Sterilised bottle, at least 250ml/10oz

To serve

- 250ml/10oz mezcal (unaged is best)
- 125ml/5oz melon syrup
- 100ml/4oz fresh, strained lemon juice
- 50ml/2oz banana liqueur
- 7.5ml/1½ tsp cider vinegar

- Funnel
- Sterilised bottle, at least 700ml/28oz
- Freshly ground black pepper, to garnish

TO MAKE THE MELON SYRUP *1.* Cut the honeydew melon flesh into chunks and put into the container with the sugar syrup. Mix together. *2.* Cover with the lid and leave to infuse in the fridge for 24 hours. Alternatively, cook the melon in the syrup sous vide for 30 minutes at 52°C/126°F, then cool (see p12). *3.* Strain through a coffee filter into the bottle (see p12). Once sealed, it can be stored in the fridge for up to 1 week.

BATCH *1.* A few hours before you want to serve, transfer all the ingredients to the bottle, seal and chill in the fridge.

JUG SERVE *1.* Once cold, it's blending time. Empty half of the cocktail from the bottle into the blender. *2.* Fill half of the blender with ice and turn it on. You will know when it is ready when you can't hear ice chunks being smashed to pieces. You're looking for a smooth, slushie-type consistency, runny enough that it will pour easily from the blender into a glass. *3.* If it is too runny add more ice and blend again; if it too thick then throw some more cocktail in and whizz it up one more time! Keep adding ice and cocktail until you have the slushie you want. *4.* Once blended, dish out the drink into chilled glasses. *5.* To garnish, you can grind a small amount of black pepper onto the top of each drink.

TIP Mezcal can be very expensive and is sometimes hard to find in shops. Your best bet is to buy it on the internet. Two good options that won't break the bank are QuiQuiRiQui Matatlan and Del Maguey Vida.

BOTTLED
MOJITO

*Do this a few days in advance of a barbecue and you can
have the best mojito you've ever drunk in your life by simply
unscrewing a lid: it's a fresh, extra-minty version of the Cuban
classic. It's very quick to prepare, and you can do it in bulk –
once made it will last a solid month, so if you have any left over
(you probably won't) you can save it for the following weekend
or the one after that.*

To bottle

– 150g/6oz caster (superfine) sugar
– 40g/1½oz fresh mint, including stalks
– 1 litre/40oz water
– 150ml/6oz light rum
– 3g/¾ tsp dried brewer's yeast
– 10g/½oz citric acid powder (see Eko Mail introduction, p44)

– Bowl, at least 1.5 litre/60oz
– Funnel
– Coffee filter
– Jug, at least 1 litre/40oz
– 6 plastic bottles, about 200ml/8oz each, with caps

To serve
– Sprigs of mint, to garnish

BOTTLE 1. In the bowl, muddle the sugar and mint together, then leave, covered, in
the fridge for 3 hours, or overnight if possible. **2.** Add the water and the rum, then stir
for 10 minutes or so to dissolve the sugar. **3.** Strain through the coffee filter into the
jug (see p12). **4.** Add the yeast and citric acid, and stir to combine. **5.** Pour the mixture
into the plastic bottles (plastic is safer for fermenting). Seal and keep in a cool place, but
not refrigerated, for 5 days or so. If you're worried about exploding bottles, use a large
plastic tub with a lid instead. **6.** If the bottles look out of shape the pressure may be
building too much. Release it by unscrewing very slowly then putting the cap back on.

7. Taste daily after 2 days. When ready it will taste minty and not too sweet, with a nice fizz. After 5 or so days, release the pressure again, and refrigerate. They will keep for 1 month, but the fresher you drink them the better they'll taste.

GLASS SERVE *1.* You can either drink this neat, or pour it over ice in a highball and garnish with mint.

EVERY CLOUD

*Everyone has either heard of or drunk plenty of the Lagerita:
it's a refreshing tequila and beer-based cocktail that is perfect for
long afternoons in the sun. Here's our take on it – we took our
favourite beer and came up with this simple and delicious long
drink that a group of our regulars refer to as the Desperado!*

To batch

– 250ml/10oz silver tequila of your choice
– 200ml/8oz fresh, strained lemon juice
– 100ml/4oz 2:1 sugar syrup (see p11)

– Jug, at least 1 litre/40oz

To serve

– Plenty of your favourite lager/pale ale/saison
– Lemon slices, to garnish

BATCH 1. Combine the tequila, lemon juice and sugar syrup in the jug. **2.** Give it a
quick stir and keep, covered, in the fridge to get it nice and cold, or until you are ready
to drink it. It will keep for 24 hours.

JUG SERVE 1. Add loads of ice to the jug and to your glassware. **2.** Pour 50ml/2oz
from the jug into each of the glasses. **3.** Top with the beer and garnish with lemon.

TIPS The beer will have a massive effect on the final flavour. A darker, hoppier beer
will create a more bitter drink, whereas a lighter, citrussy beer will lead to something
more refreshing.

Also, you can add another dimension by replacing half the volume of sugar syrup with
your preferred fruit liqueur.

AUTUMN

APPLE
& PLUM

We were asked to create a drink by a young French guy, Vincent, who makes an amazing apple-based aperitif called Trente et Quarante (30&40). Vincent's 30&40 lends itself to autumnal nights alongside other dark spirits such as whiskey and rum, but its balance inspired us to make a light, refreshing number, perfect just before dinner with friends.

This recipe uses malic acid, which occurs naturally in fruits. The powder form is the concentrate of what is found in the fruit. It can be bought online or from specialist food shops.

Bramley apple cordial

– 1kg/2lb 8oz Bramley apples (cooking apples; remove the skins if you want to try making the Rye & Dry on p142)
– Ascorbic acid (optional)
– Caster (superfine) sugar
– Malic acid (powder)

– Electric juicer
– 2 jugs or containers, at least 2 litre/80oz
– Funnel
– Coffee filter

To bottle

– 400ml/16oz 30&40 Apéritif de Normandie (for alternative, see tip on p108)
– 50ml/2oz Louis Roque La Vieille Prune (or any available French plum eau de vie)
– 25ml/1oz tomato vinegar (alternatively, 10ml/2 tsp red wine vinegar)
– 250ml/10oz Bramley apple cordial
– Sterilised bottle, at least 700ml/28oz

To serve

– Soda water
– Seasonal, edible flowers, to garnish (optional)

TO MAKE THE BRAMLEY APPLE CORDIAL *1.* Chop the Bramley apples into small enough pieces so they will fit in your juicer. No need to remove pips or stems, as they provide a great dryness to the juice. *2.* Now just juice away into one of the jugs. If you want to stop the juice browning in the jug, throw in a pinch of ascorbic acid before juicing (it will prevent oxidisation), but that's not imperative. *3.* When you're finished juicing all the apples, scoop out as much pulp as possible and strain the liquid through a coffee filter into the other jug (see p12) that is on some digital scales. *4.* Weigh the strained juice you've collected and add 80% of its weight in sugar (see p12). *5.* Stir until the sugar has dissolved. *6.* Add 20% of its new weight in malic acid. Once the malic acid has dissolved, it's ready to go. Cover and store in the fridge. It will keep for 1 month.

BOTTLE *1.* Pour the 30&40, La Vieille Prune, tomato vinegar and Bramley apple cordial into the bottle, seal and store in the fridge. This can be bottled well in advance because it keeps for 2 months.

GLASS SERVE *1.* Pour 75ml/3oz over ice in a highball glass, and top with soda water. *2.* We like to garnish with a seasonal flower to add a green, floral note – if you can catch late-summer jasmine, that's perfect.

TIPS If any of your guests aren't drinking alcohol, pour them a large measure of the Bramley apple cordial over ice in a tall glass and top with soda water. Hands down the best version of Appletiser they will ever have.

If you can't get hold of 30&40, a good calvados, cider brandy or even cognac will work really well. Just use it like for like instead of the 30&40.

STONE FENCE

Stone Fence is an alternative to the American beer-and-shot combo called the Boilermaker, using cider instead of beer, and rye whiskey as the shooter. So, as you can imagine, quite a bracing drink. We loved the idea of combining whiskey and cider but wanted to make it more accessible than just throwing back shots and downing pints. What we landed on was a drink that we feel is both complex and drinkable – it's a favourite sharpener for us on a busy evening in the bar.

To batch
– 100ml/4oz of your preferred American whiskey
– 40ml/1½oz good-quality peach liqueur
– 40ml/1½oz 2:1 sugar syrup (see p11)
– 100ml/4oz fresh, strained lemon juice
– 2.5ml/½ tsp Angostura bitters
– 360ml/14½oz water
– 180ml/7¼oz dry cider

– Jug or bowl, at least 1 litre/40oz
– Funnel
– Soda siphon/cream whipper
– NO₂ canister

BATCH *1.* Add the ingredients to the jug and stir to mix together. *2.* Pour through the funnel into the siphon. *3.* Charge with one canister of NO₂ (see p11), shake and leave to settle in the fridge until you are ready to drink it. It will keep for 36 hours.

GLASS SERVE *1.* When ready, slowly release the gas using the lever. Don't pull the lever all the way down, otherwise you and your kitchen will be covered in drink. Pull the lever until you start to hear a hissing sound, and hold until it stops. *2.* Unscrew the top and pour the drink into tumbler glasses, rather than using the nozzle. This will give you a lighter drink, rather than a frothy one.

TIP You can swap the liqueur for any fruit liqueur you prefer. American whiskies get on well with stone fruit liqueurs, such as apricot. A heavily rye-based whiskey is good here.

'WINE'

*Why is this called 'Wine'? Because it has some of the tannic feel
of a normal wine, but is actually non-alcoholic – ideal if you've
overdone it and need a night off. It may be a challenge to get hold
of grains of selim, which have an amazing smoky, umami note.
If so swap them out for lapsang souchong tea or clove. Birch leaf
is available online and supplies a woody depth, but isn't essential.*

To bottle

- 10g/½oz dried hibiscus
- 2 seeds of grains of selim (or 3g/1½ tsp lapsang souchong tea,
  or 1 clove)
- 2g/1¼ tsp whole allspice
- 1g/½ tsp birch leaf
- 80g/3¼oz sliced strawberries
- 80g/3¼oz sliced cherries (including stones)
- 40g/1½oz sliced blackberries
- 1g/½ tsp jasmine silver-tip tea
- 800ml/32oz 100% pressed white grape juice

- Cooking thermometer
- Coffee filter
- Funnel
- 2 x sterilised bottles, at least 1 litre/40oz

BOTTLE *1.* First things first. Measure out all the spices, fruits and tea, and set them
to one side. *2.* Next add the grape juice to a saucepan. *3.* Place over a low–medium
heat. Using the thermometer, bring the grape juice up to 50–55°C/122–131°F.
4. Once at the desired temperature add all the spices, fruits and tea and cook for
30 minutes, making sure the temperature doesn't go above 55°C/131°F. Alternatively,
cook sous vide for 30 minutes at 60°C/140°F (see p12). *5.* Once you have cooked
the liquid, strain it through a coffee filter into the jug (see p12) that is on some digital
scales. *6.* When you have a weight for the strained liquid, add the same weight in
filtered, still water (see p12). *7.* Give the mixture a good stir to combine then pour into
the bottles, seal and store in the fridge. It will keep for 2 weeks.

GLASS SERVE When the liquid is nice and chilled, grab some glasses and pour.

PARADISE
MARTINI

Okra in a cocktail? Yes! Okra is popular in parts of Africa, South Asia and the US Deep South, and as well as having a unique, vegetal taste, it releases a thickening agent that gives this Martini a very interesting texture. It actually makes it seem colder than it is and allows it to stand up to spicy foods – so this is a fine alternative to wine or beer at a dinner party. Grains of paradise is a pepper-like spice from the ginger family, native to West Africa. It's readily available from specialist food shops.

To make the grains of paradise gin

– 45g/1¾oz grains of paradise
– 450ml/18oz London dry gin

– Kilner jar or similar airtight, non-reactive container, at least 500ml/20oz
– Funnel
– Coffee filter
– Sterilised bottle, at least 500ml/20oz

To make the okra-infused vermouth

– 25g/1oz okra
– 100ml/4oz dry vermouth
– 75g/3oz caster (superfine) sugar

– Kilner jar or similar airtight, non-reactive container, at least 200ml/8oz
– Funnel
– Sterilised bottle, at least 200ml/8oz

To bottle

– 450ml/18oz grains of paradise gin
– 100ml/4oz okra-infused vermouth
– 150ml/6oz water

– Jug, at least 700ml/28oz
– Funnel
– Sterilised bottle, at least 700ml/28oz

To serve

– Nasturtium leaves, or slice of okra, to garnish

TO MAKE THE GRAINS OF PARADISE GIN *1.* Put the grains of paradise in the Kilner jar. *2.* Pour the gin into the jar and seal it, then give it a quick shake. *3.* Leave to infuse for 24 hours. *4.* Alternatively, cook sous vide for 30 minutes at 52°C/126°F (see p12). *5.* Once infused, strain through a coffee filter into the bottle (see p12).

TO MAKE THE OKRA-INFUSED VERMOUTH *1.* Finely slice the okra and chuck it into the Kilner jar. *2.* Add the dry vermouth. (If you've opened a new bottle for this you might have some vermouth left over – don't throw it away, it is amazing to add to sauces instead of white wine when cooking.) *3.* Seal the Kilner jar shut then give it a shake and leave to infuse for 24 hours. Alternatively, cook sous vide for 30 minutes at 52°C/126°F (see p12) *4.* After it has infused, strain the vermouth through a sieve into a jug. *5.* Add the sugar and stir until all the sugar has dissolved, then pour into the bottle and seal. *6.* Store in the fridge until ready to use. It will keep for 2 weeks. *7.* You will have noticed that the vermouth has thickened and become, for want of a better word, syrupy. Don't worry, this is normal – when sliced, okra releases a substance that thickens any liquid it is cooked or infused into.

BOTTLE *1.* Pour the measured gin, okra vermouth and water into the jug. Give it a stir to combine everything. *2.* Pour into the bottle. *3.* Seal the bottle and store in the fridge or freezer until ready to serve. It will keep for 1 month.

GLASS SERVE *1.* Grab a few Martini or coupette glasses and just pour your desired amount into each glass. *2.* To garnish, drop in a slice of okra. Or float a nasturtium leaf on top of each drink. *3.* For an easy yet special extra touch, use a teaspoon to place a single drop of the drink onto the nasturtium leaf.

AVRIL

This was the first drink we put on our menu that used an alternative source of acidity – fermented pear syrup – to the usual lemon or lime juice. The combination of that syrup, Martini Rubino and amontillado sherry gives an incredible autumnal feel to a tall, refreshing drink.

Fermented pear syrup

– 200g/8oz Williams pears
– 5g/1¼ tsp White Labs dried saison yeast (or another saison yeast)
– 1 litre/40oz water
– Caster (superfine) sugar
– Citric acid powder (see Eko Mail introduction, p44)
– Kilner jar or similar airtight, non-reactive container, at least 1.5 litre/60oz
– Cheesecloth or clean tea towel (dish towel)
– Funnel
– Coffee filter
– Jug, at least 1.5 litre/60oz

To batch

– 200ml/8oz good-quality vodka
– 200ml/8oz Martini Riserva Speciale Rubino (for alternative, see tip on p122)
– 150ml/6oz fermented pear syrup
– 100ml/4oz amontillado sherry
– 100ml/4oz Minus 8 Red Verjus (see Eko Mail introduction, p45)
– Jug, at least 1 litre/40oz

To serve

– Soda water
– Long pieces of lemon zest, to garnish

TO MAKE THE FERMENTED PEAR SYRUP *1.* Start by chopping up the pears into small chunks or quarters. *2.* Add the pears, peel and core included, to the Kilner jar along with the yeast and water and give it a stir. *3.* Cover with a cheesecloth or tea towel and seal the lid over the cloth. *4.* Store in a dark place. *5.* Leave for 5–7 days to ferment, tasting daily after 2 days. You will know when it is ready when the juice has a complex sweet and acidic pear quality to it. As with other fermented recipes in this book, taste regularly to avoid over-fermentation. Stop if any overly acidic or 'off' flavours make themselves known. *6.* Once you have the flavour profile you want, strain it through a coffee filter into the jug (see p12) that is on some digital scales. *7.* Weigh the juice and add the same weight of sugar (see p12). *8.* Stir to dissolve the sugar – it can take a while, so feel free to stir in fits and bursts. *9.* Weigh the syrup, then add citric acid to taste. A good starting point is 5% citric acid, then work up until you have a good balance of sweetness and acidity.

BATCH *1.* Combine all the ingredients in the jug. If batching ahead, cover and stick the mix in the fridge. It will keep for 1 month.

TO SERVE *1.* When you're ready to serve, fill the jug with ice. Take your glasses of choice and fill them with ice. *2.* Add 75ml/3oz of the mix from the jug to each and then top with chilled soda water. *3.* Give the drinks a quick stir. *4.* Take a long strip of lemon zest and squeeze the oil from the skin over the top of each drink. Slide the zest down the side of the glass with the skin facing outward.

TIP If you cannot get hold of Martini Riserva Speciale Rubino, pick another good-quality sweet or red vermouth. Every brand, with its different botanicals, will add its own complexity to the drink.

YUZU NEGRONI

MARCIS DZELZAINIS, SAGER + WILDE, LONDON, UK

Marcis is almost definitely the most talented person we have in our industry in London: at times he's run such bars as Dandelyan, 69 Colebrooke Row, Satan's Whiskers and Sager + Wilde. If he shouted a little louder about his talents he would be better known outside the industry, but that's part of what makes him such a good person to have a drink with. Max worked with Marcis for a couple of years earlier in his career. His drink is one of only a couple of Negroni variations that are better than the untampered-with original. Yuzu sake is made with a perfumed Japanese citrus and adds a floral aroma, and the mix of Campari and Punt e Mes aperitifs bring a full, rounded bitterness.

To bottle

– 160ml/6½oz gin
– 160ml/6½oz yuzu sake
– 160ml/6½oz Campari
– 90ml/3¾oz Punt e Mes
– 140ml/5½oz water

– Jug or container, at least 750ml/30oz
– Funnel
– Sterilised bottle, at least 750ml/30oz

BOTTLE 1. So easy. Mix all the ingredients together in the jug. **2.** Transfer to the bottle. It can be stored in fridge for up to 1 year, but it's better in the freezer: because of the alcohol and sugar content, it won't freeze.

GLASS SERVE 1. Serve over ice in a rocks glass. Thanks, Marcis!

WEDDING HIP FLASK

This cocktail is a godsend for any sort of extended occasion, like a countryside ramble or a day at the races. At weddings there's often a lot of waiting around (even if it's you who's getting married!). A hip flask is a reliable way to keep a few people going during the slow bits. What's more, you can take it to a whole summer of weddings, as its flavour slowly becomes deeper and richer as it matures with age.

The sweet French aperitif Dubonnet is underrated: it brings so much depth to drinks and that's why we love it. This makes enough to fill a normal-sized hip flask.

To batch

- 150ml/6oz decent whisk(e)y – Glenfarclas 10 Year Old for Max, Michter's US*1 rye for Noel
- 50ml/2oz Dubonnet
- 5ml/1 tsp Benedictine
- Zest of 1 small orange

- Jug or container, at least 250ml/10oz
- Funnel
- Hip flask

BATCH *1.* Put all the ingredients into the jug. *2.* Zest the orange and squeeze the oils from the peel over the top of the liquid, then stir to combine. *3.* Pour into your hip flask. It will last a good long while – up to 1 year in the flask.

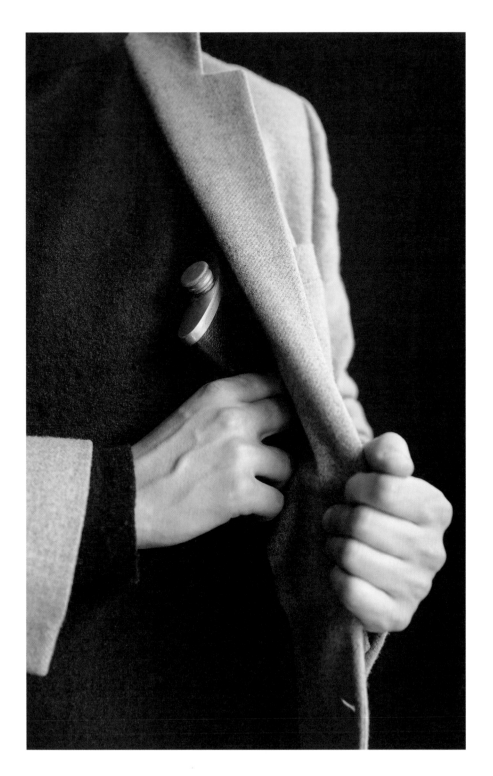

FIG NEGRONI

A great seasonal take on the Negroni using early autumn figs.
The richness of the fig vermouth married with the perfume of the
fig leaf gin creates subtle complexity and a Negroni that is slightly
softer than the traditional version. Serve your guests small glasses
at the start of a dinner party, or pour yourself a big glass after
a tough day in the office.

To bottle
- 100g/4oz fresh figs
- 250ml/10oz sweet vermouth
- 30g/1¼oz fig leaves
- 250ml/10oz gin
- 250ml/10oz Campari

- 3 jugs or containers, at least 1 litre/40oz
- Funnel
- Coffee filter
- Sterilised bottle, at least 1 litre/40oz

To serve
- Orange slices, to garnish

BOTTLE *1.* Quarter the figs, and add them to the jug with the vermouth. *2.* Leave to infuse, covered, for 24 hours in a cool place. Alternatively, cook sous vide for 30 minutes at 40°C/104°F, then cool (see p12). *3.* Slice the fig leaves lengthways and combine with the gin in the second jug. *4.* Leave to infuse, covered, in a cool place for 24–48 hours, depending on how 'figgy' you want it – sniff regularly. Alternatively, cook sous vide for 45 minutes at 40°C/104°F, then cool. *5.* Strain the vermouth and gin through a coffee filter into the third jug (see p12). *6.* Add the Campari, then transfer to a bottle, seal and store in the fridge. It will keep for 2 months.

GLASS SERVE *1.* Simply pour 75ml/3oz over ice into your glass of choice.

TIP Don't buy figs if you don't have to – wait for the season and find a tree (we have so many near us in the centre of London). If there are no fig trees to be seen try this with the same weight of blackcurrants and their leaves instead. They grow *everywhere*.

MALTS, OATS & LEAF

This drink is basically a twist on a traditional whisky sour with a much fuller mouthfeel from the oat milk, and a floral finish provided by the manuka leaf (a flowering plant native to Australia and New Zealand). Tinctures are a great way to extract flavour and they last a long time. You can add a little bit of tincture to a sugar source, be it honey or syrup, and then use that as a base for any cocktail calling for sweetness – it works very well in a Tom Collins (gin, lemon juice and sugar, topped with soda in a long glass over ice).

Manuka tincture

- 50ml/2oz vodka
- 8g/3 tsp dried manuka leaf

- Clean, empty jam jar with a lid, or similar lidded container
- Funnel
- Coffee filter
- Sterilised bottle, at least 50ml/2oz

To batch

- 350ml/14oz blended Scotch whisky (try Monkey Shoulder)
- 200ml/8oz fresh, strained lemon juice
- 125ml/5oz oat milk (Oatly is a great brand)
- 100g/4oz honey
- 100ml/4oz water
- 10ml/2 tsp manuka tincture

- Jug or container, at least 1 litre/40oz
- Soda siphon/cream whipper
- NO₂ cartridge

TO MAKE THE MANUKA TINCTURE *1.* Put the vodka and manuka leaf in the jar, seal and leave to steep overnight. Or cook sous vide for 30 minutes at 52.5°C/127°F, then cool (see p12). *2.* Strain off the leaves through the coffee filter into the bottle (see p12). Once sealed, the tincture will keep for years in a cool dark place.

BATCH *1.* Add all the ingredients to the jug and stir to combine. *2.* Pour into the soda siphon and charge with an NO₂ canister (see p11). *3.* Shake the siphon to distribute the gas. *4.* Chill for at least 3 hours in the fridge. If you don't want to serve it straight away, it will keep uncharged for 1 week.

GLASS SERVE *1.* When ready to serve, invert the siphon and squeeze the nozzle gently. *2.* Split the mixture between the glasses, to about three-quarters full, and allow to settle, then top up to fill the glasses.

TIP If you don't have a soda siphon, you can make this with a cocktail shaker instead. Put 150ml/6oz of the mix into the shaker. Fill with ice and shake, strain, drink.

HIDDEN
MARTINI

*Sometimes you need the simplicity and instant hit of a Martini.
The long exhale at the end of a trying day. Unfortunately, at
home we don't always have the tools, time or energy. This one
can stay hidden in the freezer and is for just that occasion.
Simply drop an olive in or zest a lemon on the top and breathe.*

To bottle

- 450ml/18oz gin
- 125ml/5oz dry vermouth
- 160ml/6¹/₂oz water (use bottled if you have it in the house)
- Funnel
- Sterilised bottle, at least 750ml/30oz

To serve

- Green olives or lemon zests, to garnish

BOTTLE *1.* Use the funnel to pour all the ingredients into the bottle, seal and shake
gently to mix. ***2.*** Store in the freezer. It will keep indefinitely.

GLASS SERVE *1.* Fill a cocktail glass, choose your garnish.

WINTER

SHISO MISO

Fat-washing is a great way of adding another dimension to spirits, giving them incredible depth. When flavour from fat in liquid form is mixed with alcohol, aroma molecules transfer into the alcohol part of the liquid. The fat also imparts some of its own flavour.

Get this prepped and kept in a bottle in the fridge to enjoy one before (and probably after) dinner.

Fat-washed whisky

– 450ml/18oz Nikka All Malt or another good malty whisky
– 75g/3oz unsalted butter
– 6g/⅓oz fresh shiso leaves (a leaf from the mint family, widely used in Asian cooking)
– 6g/⅓oz white miso paste

– 2 jugs or plastic containers, at least 500ml/20oz
– Funnel
– Coffee filter

To bottle

– 400ml/16oz fat-washed whisky (this volume is likely to be all you have, as you'll lose about 50ml/2oz from the washing process)
– 100ml/4oz unwashed whisky
– 100ml/4oz 2:1 sugar syrup (see p11)
– 25ml/1oz Angostura bitters
– 300ml/12oz chilled water

– Jug or bowl, at least 1.5 litre/60oz
– Sterilised bottle, at least 1.5 litre/60oz

To serve

– Shiso leaves, to garnish

TO MAKE THE FAT-WASHED WHISKY *1.* Put your whisky of choice into one of the jugs. *2.* Cut the butter into small chunks (so it melts evenly) and place in a saucepan over a medium heat. Allow the butter to fully melt. *3.* Once melted, add the shiso leaves and miso paste and stir into the butter. Cook for a few minutes until the butter starts to brown, then remove from heat. *4.* Pour the mixture into the whisky and stir to combine everything. *5.* Place cling film (plastic wrap) tightly over the top. *6.* Place in the freezer overnight or until all the butter has risen to the top and frozen into a solid disc. *7.* Strain through a coffee filter into the other jug (see p12). The disc of butter will be left in the filter.

BOTTLE *1.* Put all the ingredients into the jug and stir to combine. *2.* Transfer to a bottle, seal and store in the fridge. It keeps for 3 months.

GLASS SERVE *1.* Simply grab as many glasses as you need, add ice and pour from the bottle. *2.* Garnish with a shiso leaf.

139

BLOODY MARY

This is an opportunity to use up bits of veg from the fridge, as it starts with a basic sofrito – an Italian mix of diced vegetables. This recipe also calls for stock: if no vegetarians are around, chicken stock will create a Bloody Mary like none you've ever had before. Vegetable stock is okay too, but it lacks fat so it won't have the same depth. If you have friends staying over, prepare it the night before. Then the morning after you can focus on the bacon butties, and pour this straight into a glass, or over vodka if it's that sort of morning after. It's more work, yes, but guaranteed to be the finest Bloody Mary you'll ever drink.

Spiced tomato mix

- 25g/1oz butter or olive oil
- 200g/8oz assorted vegetables (carrot, onion, celery, potato etc)
- 1–3 fresh chillies – go as hot as you like!
- Salt and pepper, to taste
- ½ tsp smoked paprika
- 1 stock cube (chicken or veg; we prefer the jellied stock pots)
- 1 tbsp tomato paste
- 50ml/2oz Worcestershire sauce
- 25ml/1oz red wine vinegar
- 700ml/28oz good-quality tomato juice

- Jug, at least 1 litre/40oz
- Funnel
- Sterilised bottle, at least 1 litre/40oz

To serve

- Your alcohol(s) of choice
- Spiced tomato mix
- Celery leaves, to garnish

TO MAKE THE SPICED TOMATO MIX *1.* Gently heat the butter or oil in a frying pan. *2.* Finely dice the veg and the chilli. *3.* Fry over a medium–low heat until softened, about 15 minutes, as if you were making the base for a sauce. *4.* Season with salt, pepper and the smoked paprika. Add the stock cube, tomato paste, Worcestershire sauce and vinegar. *5.* Stir together and cook for another minute or so. If it seems dry add a splash of water. *6.* Take off the heat and stir in the tomato juice. *7.* Pass through a sieve into the jug, then transfer to the bottle. Once cooled, store it in the fridge. It will keep for 48 hours.

GLASS SERVE

1. Fill a glass with ice, then pour in 25ml/1oz spirit of your choice. Vodka works along with a splash of port, as does gin with red wine. Or tequila and the cocktail served next to a beer, if it's a bad hangover. *2.* Top with the spiced tomato mix and garnish.

RYE & DRY

We took inspiration from the classic Rye and Dry (rye and ginger ale) to make this one. Tall and refreshing, it showcases another aspect of what can be done with whiskey in cocktails. It uses the apple cordial from the Apple & Plum (see p106), but the end result is drier on the palate.

Apple skin-infused rye whiskey

− 2 Bramley apples, skins only
− 500ml/20oz rye whiskey

− Kilner jar or similar airtight, non-reactive container, at least 1 litre/40oz
− Jug, at least 750ml/30oz
− Funnel
− Sterilised bottle, at least 750ml/30oz

To batch

− 500ml/20oz apple skin-infused rye whiskey
− 250ml/10oz Bramley apple cordial (see p106)
− 5ml/1 tsp Angostura bitters

− Sterilised bottle, at least 1 litre/40oz

To serve

− Soda water
− Lemon slices, to garnish

TO MAKE THE APPLE SKIN-INFUSED RYE WHISKEY *1.* Peel the skins from Bramley apples. Keep the flesh from the apples as they can be used in the Bramley apple cordial (see p106). *2.* Add the skins and whiskey to the Kilner jar. *3.* Let it steep for between 6 hours and overnight. *4.* Taste the whiskey – it should have a fresh apple characteristic. If not, don't worry: just let it steep a while longer. *5.* Strain the whiskey through a sieve into the jug (see p12) and then transfer to the bottle. Seal and store somewhere cool. It will keep for 6 months.

BATCH *1.* Add the apple skin-infused rye whiskey to the bottle along with the Bramley apple cordial and Angostura bitters. *2.* Seal and put in the fridge until ready to serve. It will keep for 3 months.

GLASS SERVE *1.* When the time comes to serve, add ice to a number of tall glasses. *2.* Pour 50ml/2oz cocktail into each. *3.* Top with chilled soda water. *4.* Garnish with a slice of lemon.

WINTER

143

WHISKY SODA

When Max was at university in Edinburgh he loved drinking Scotch and cream soda before a night out. So, we decided to bring some nostalgia to our bar by recreating it in a more appealing, grown-up way for our customers. Essentially, we make a milk punch flavoured with vanilla and top it with soda water. It has become one of the most popular drinks we've ever put on our menu.

What's a milk punch? It's an old way of clarifying and softening harsh booze, and it was championed by none other than Founding Father Benjamin Franklin. Milk punches have silky, soft, round flavours. We would recommend giving yourself plenty of time to prep this one by starting the day before you want to serve it.

WINTER

Whisky milk punch

- 300ml/12oz blended Scotch whisky, plus 100ml /4oz
- 100ml/4oz fresh, unstrained lemon juice (you need the sediment left in)
- 150ml/6oz whole milk
- 200g/8oz caster (superfine) sugar
- 1ml/dash vanilla extract
- 4g/scant ½ tsp citric acid

- 3 jugs, at least 1 litre/40oz
- Funnel
- Coffee filter
- Sterilised bottle, at least 1 litre/40oz bottle

To serve

- Chilled soda water
- Lemon slices, to garnish

TO MAKE THE WHISKY MILK PUNCH *1.* Bear with us on this one. It does get quite detailed, but the results are well worth it. Mix the 300ml/12oz Scotch and lemon together in one of the jugs. *2.* Put the milk in another jug. Then pour the Scotch and lemon mixture into the milk. You should start to see large, cloud-like curds forming straight away. *3.* Cover with cling film (plastic wrap) and leave it to rest in the fridge for 2 hours. *4.* After 2 hours, set up a funnel and coffee filter over the other jug and strain the mixture (see p12). This step can take a long time, so we recommend setting it up in the fridge and leaving it overnight. *5.* Sometimes the first strain does not produce the crystal-clear whisky you want. If this is the case, just pass the strained liquid through the same coffee filter you used first time, and it will be clear when you come back to it. *6.* The next step is to add flavour and balance to the milk punch. Add the sugar, vanilla, citric acid and remaining 100ml/4oz of Scotch. *7.* Stir until everything has dissolved and been well combined. *8.* Transfer to the bottle and seal. It will keep in the fridge for up to 1 year.

GLASS SERVE *1.* OK. The complicated bit is over. Grab some tall glasses and pack them with ice. *2.* Pour in a large measure of the whisky milk punch and top with soda water. *3.* Give it a quick stir to combine, then garnish each with a slice of lemon.

TIPS You can add other flavours to the milk punch, those that team up well with whisky and vanilla. Spices such as cinnamon and nutmeg are surefire winners. If you're feeling truly adventurous you can throw in some chilli to add a kick. We always suggest starting with small amounts and working your way up until you get the desired results.

If whisky is not your dark spirit of choice this recipe will also work well with rum, cognac or calvados.

WINTER

MASTIC

Mastic is an evocative flavour from the Mediterranean,
specifically Greece and Turkey, where Max spent a week working
with bartenders along the Aegean coast. It is a resin from a tree
of the same name and has been used as a flavouring for centuries;
it has a floral yet woody aroma, and is slightly piney. (You can
buy it from a specialist food shop, or instead use a different spice
– cardamom is a good one.) We wanted to create a long drink
that mimicked a vodka soda, with a little more body and some
perfumed notes drifting through. It's a real refresher and perfect
to bottle, chill and grab when leaving the house on the way to
a party.

Mastic vodka
- 500ml/20oz vodka
- 7.5g/scant tbsp gum mastic
- 125g/5oz caster (superfine) sugar
- 2g/½ tsp citric acid powder (see Eko Mail introduction, p44)
- 1g/¼ tsp malic acid
- Jug or container, at least 750ml/30oz
- Funnel
- Coffee filter
- Sterilised bottle, at least 750ml/30oz

To bottle and serve
- Chilled mastic vodka
- Chilled small bottles of soda water, one for each drink you
  want to make

TO MAKE THE MASTIC VODKA 1. Put all the ingredients in the jug and stir to
dissolve the sugar. **2.** Then either cover and leave the ingredients to infuse for 24 hours,
or cook sous vide for 30 minutes at 53°C/127°F (see p12). Leave to cool. **3.** Strain off
the mastic (you can dry this out and reuse it) by pouring through a coffee filter into a
bottle (see p12). Seal and store the mastic vodka for up to 6 months in the fridge.

BOTTLE *1.* Carefully pour out 50ml/2oz of soda water from one of the bottles. *2.* Replace with 50ml/2oz cold mastic vodka, carefully, in order to keep the soda water as fizzy as possible. Make sure there is as little air as possible at the top of the bottle. *3.* Push the cap back on. *4.* Repeat as many times as you need to. *5.* Get these guys as cold as possible and consume within a week. *6.* They won't go off, but they will go flat. To serve, just crack them open!

WINTER

151

PLANTAIN OLD FASHIONED

WINTER

This cocktail uses fat-washing like in the Shiso Miso (see p136), but it's on the sweeter side, so it's perfect to drink after dinner as an alternative to whisky or other digestif. It's also a good partner to hard cheeses such as Cheddar or Comté. In fact, you won't need any chutney – the drink will provide the sweetness. We love using plantain, which is so plentiful in shops in our pocket of east London.

Plantain rum

- 500ml/20oz golden rum
- 100g/4oz unsalted butter
- 8g/⅓oz barley miso paste (from a Japanese grocery shop or big supermarket, or substitute for any other miso paste)
- 60g/2½oz plantain, peeled and sliced

- Jug or bowl, at least 750ml/30oz
- Funnel
- Coffee filter
- Sterilised bottle, at least 700ml/28oz

To bottle

- 400ml/16oz plantain rum
- 100ml/4oz 2:1 sugar syrup (see p11)
- 5ml/1 tsp Angostura bitters
- 200ml/8oz water

- Jug, at least 750ml/30oz
- Funnel
- Sterilised bottle, at least 750ml/30oz

TO MAKE THE PLANTAIN RUM *1.* Put the golden rum into the jug and set aside. *2.* Measure out the rest of your ingredients so that you're ready to go. *3.* Put the unsalted butter in a frying pan and melt it on a medium heat. *4.* Once the butter has melted, add the barley miso paste and stir it in. *5.* Next add the slices of plantain and fry in the butter until golden and the butter starts to brown. *6.* Pour the contents of the frying pan into the jug with the rum in and give it a quick stir. Seal the jug with cling film (plastic wrap) and put it in the freezer overnight. *7.* The next day, pull the jug out: there should be a solid disc of butter above the rum. If not, no worries, just put back in the freezer for another 6 hours to make sure all the butter solidifies. *8.* Once you have a solid disc of butter, strain the rum through a coffee filter into the bottle (see p12). The disc will be left in the filter. Seal the bottle and store somewhere cool. It will keep for 3 months.

BOTTLE *1.* Pour the plantain rum, sugar syrup, Angostura bitters and water into the jug. *2.* Give it a quick stir to combine, then pour through the funnel into the bottle and seal. Store in the fridge. It will keep for 3 months.

GLASS SERVE *1.* Grab some glasses or stoneware cups and fill with ice. *2.* Pour the Plantain Old Fashioned into the vessels.

15 SECOND OLD FASHIONED

Max used to work in a small bar in Manchester that got incredibly busy at the weekends, and the drink of choice was the Old Fashioned. At that time the custom was to make them one by one, with granulated sugar stirred into bourbon whiskey for ten minutes or so to dissolve it. Not only did this massively over-dilute the drink, it was also painfully slow when the place was rammed. Here's our modern version – we wanted a quicker way to make this but without compromising on the quality of what is a robust classic. Rooibos adds a tremendous depth of flavour and some aromatic notes.

To bottle

- 200ml/8oz boiling water
- 3g/1½ tsp rooibos tea leaves
- 75g/3oz demerara sugar
- 500ml/20oz bourbon (Woodford Reserve is our choice)
- 10ml/2 tsp Angostura bitters

- Funnel
- Coffee filter
- Jug or container, at least 1 litre/40oz
- Sterilised bottle, at least 1 litre/40oz

BOTTLE *1.* Pour the boiling water over the rooibos in a jug or teapot and leave to infuse for 10 minutes. This may seem like a long time, but it will pull some tannins from the tea, which is brilliant for the final drink. *2.* Strain off the leaves through a coffee filter into the jug (see p12). *3.* Add the sugar and stir to dissolve, then leave to cool. *4.* Add the bourbon and bitters. *5.* Transfer to the bottle, seal and store in the fridge. It will keep for 6 months.

GLASS SERVE Pour 100ml/4oz over ice into whisky glasses.

TIP Swap the spirit, or try with another tea. Jasmine tea will work with lighter spirits, for example, like gin or tequila. Or Earl Grey with a light Scotch, like Old Pulteney 12.

WINTER

157

HOT
CHOCOLATE

A winter warmer, and a brilliant drink to take your time over.
This is indulgent and rich, and perfect after a long winter walk or
a chilly afternoon at the football. The addition of a roux provides
a great texture without the powdery taste you would get from the
cornflour (cornstarch) commonly used in hot chocolate.

To batch

– 25g/1oz butter
– 25g/1oz plain flour
– 500ml/20oz milk
– 1 bay leaf
– 1 clove
– 5 black peppercorns
– 60g/2¹⁄₂oz honey
– 300g/12oz good-quality chocolate, finely diced
– 30g/1¹⁄₄oz cocoa powder
– 150ml/6oz Scotch whisky, cognac or other dark spirit

BATCH *1.* First, make the roux. Melt the butter in a saucepan over a medium heat and add the flour. *2.* Cook for a couple of minutes, stirring. A roux can 'break' if you don't make it very carefully and slowly! *3.* Add the milk a little at a time, and once you have added half of it, add the bay leaf, clove, black peppercorns and honey. *4.* Continue stirring, adding the rest of the milk and cook until it has the consistency of a runny custard. *5.* At this point take it off the heat, add the chocolate and stir until it melts. *6.* Stir in the cocoa powder, add the alcohol and you are ready to serve. This can also be pre-prepared and stored in the fridge, then reheated within 48 hours. Just get it back to about 70°C/158°F. *7.* To serve, just ladle it straight from the pan into warmed mugs or heavy glasses.

TIP If you want to take this somewhere frosty in a flask, add boiling water to the flask to warm, and bring the finished mix back up to just below boiling temperature. Discard the water and fill the flask. Best sipped on the top of a hill with a view.

GRAPE OLD FASHIONED

We created this drink for a pop-up we did at a pub down the road from our bar called The Haggerston, a late-night place with a party atmosphere. It's a less reverential, more quaffable version of the classic Old Fashioned that's easier to drink at 1am. Serve yours when the party is rolling.

Red grape syrup

– 500g/20oz red grapes
– 200ml/8oz water
– Caster (superfine) sugar

– 2 large mixing bowls or jugs
– Funnel
– Coffee filter
– Sterilised bottle, at least 500ml/20oz

To bottle

– 500ml/20oz gin
– 100ml/4oz red grape syrup
– 5ml/1 tsp Angostura bitters
– 200ml/8oz water

– Sterilised bottle, at least 1 litre/40oz

To serve

– Lemons, to garnish

TO MAKE THE RED GRAPE SYRUP

1. Add the grapes and water to a pan and heat on a medium heat until simmering. *2.* Simmer for 10 minutes or until the skins on the grapes start separating from the flesh. *3.* Pour the entire contents of the pan through a sieve into one of the jugs, pressing down on the grapes to extract all the juice. *4.* Strain this liquid through a coffee filter into the other jug (see p12) that is on some digital scales. *5.* Weigh this juice and add 200% of the weight of juice in sugar (see p12). Dissolving the sugar is going to take a while, so stir at regular intervals until there is no sugar visible. *6.* Transfer the syrup to the bottle and seal. It will keep in the fridge for up to 2 months. *7.* Here's an alternative method, if you have a good electric juicer, like a centrifugal juicer: juice the grapes through the machine, strain the liquid through a coffee filter and add double (200%) the amount of caster sugar to the strained weight of the juice.

BOTTLE *1.* Pour all the ingredients into the bottle, seal and store in the fridge. It will keep indefinitely, so you can make larger batches if you want.

GLASS SERVE *1.* Fill a rocks glass or tumbler with ice and pour 100ml/4oz of the cocktail into the glass. *2.* For each drink, take a lemon and using a peeler or sharp knife, cut off a long strip of the zest. *3.* Squeeze to express the oils over the drink, dropping the zest in afterward.

TIP If you want a quick way to make grape syrup, buy a good-quality, not-from-concentrate red or white grape juice and add 2 parts sugar to 1 part juice by weight, and stir until dissolved.

BARLEY HIGHBALL

This is a perfect winter drink, but can be made all year round as it uses dried barley. It can be an interesting soft drink or combined with a spirit of your choice. It takes us back to the fruit barley water of our childhood – but with a splash of peach liqueur it becomes something a bit more adult.

Barley water

– 100g/4oz pearl barley
– 900ml/36oz water
– 2g/½ tsp citric acid powder (see Eko Mail introduction, p44)
– 50g/2oz caster (superfine) sugar

– 2 jugs or containers, at least 2 litre/80oz
– Funnel
– Coffee filter

To serve

– 25ml/1oz spirit or liqueur per serve – peach liqueur makes for a gently fruity long drink, or Japanese whiskey turns it into a more serious pre-dinner aperitif
– 100ml/4oz (approximately) barley water per serve

TO MAKE THE BARLEY WATER *1.* Add all the ingredients to one of the jugs and stir to combine. *2.* Leave it for 24 hours, covered, in a cool place. *3.* Strain through a coffee filter into the other jug (see p12). Keep it covered in the fridge for up to 1 week.

GLASS SERVE *1.* Pour the alcohol into a glass over ice. *2.* Top with the barley water. *3.* Or simply serve the barley water over ice with a splash of soda water for a complex and refreshing non-alcoholic drink.

COSMO

The Cosmopolitan was trendy for so long, but it's maybe not as cool as it used to be. Cocktails go in and out of fashion like clothes. The quality of the cranberry is what makes the difference here, so if you wait for its season you can get some amazing fruit. This drink is a sophisticated but straightforward update, with fermented cranberry and gentle orange flower water – it's ideal before a night out and equally good as a nightcap.

Fermented cranberry cordial

- 500g/20oz fresh cranberries (frozen if fresh are unavailable)
- 3g/¾ tsp brewer's yeast (go for something light here, a saison or pilsner strain)
- 500ml/20oz water
- Caster (superfine) sugar
- Citric acid powder (see Eko Mail introduction, p44)

- Kilner jar or similar airtight, non-reactive container, at least 2 litre/80oz
- Cheesecloth or clean tea towel (dish towel)
- Elastic band
- Funnel
- Coffee filter
- Jug, at least 1 litre/40oz
- Sterilised bottle, at least 1 litre/40oz

To bottle

- 300ml/12oz vodka
- 175ml/7oz fermented cranberry cordial
- 175ml/7oz water
- 50ml/2oz triple sec
- 2ml/½ tsp orange flower water

- Sterilised bottle, at least 700ml/28oz

To serve

- Orange zests, to garnish

TO MAKE THE FERMENTED CRANBERRY CORDIAL *1.* Put the cranberries in the Kilner jar with the yeast and water, and give it a stir. *2.* Cover with the cheesecloth or tea towel and secure with the elastic band. Leave in a dark dry place for 5–7 days to ferment. *3.* After 2 days, taste daily. If you detect any vinegary or 'off' flavours, it's time to stop. Once the liquid is a little fizzy and tastes tart and juicy, strain the liquid through a coffee filter into the jug (see p12) that is on some digital scales. *4.* Weigh the fermented juice (see p12) and add the sugar at 60% of the weight of the juice. Then add citric acid at 0.5% of the original weight of the juice. This helps stabilise the fermented cordial. *5.* Stir until the sugar and citric acid have dissolved. *6.* Transfer to the bottle and seal. It will keep in the fridge for 1 month.

BOTTLE *1.* Add all the ingredients to the bottle and seal. *2.* Shake gently to mix, then store in the freezer. It will keep for 3 months.

GLASS SERVE Pour into a cocktail glass and flame with an orange zest. To flame the zest, cut a 10p-sized disc (about a US quarter) of orange zest and hold it between your thumb and forefinger. Warm the dimpled side with a lighter, then squeeze the peel side forward to expel the oils through the flame onto the top of the liquid. There you have it, you're in a trendy bar in 2006.

WINTER

COFFEE &
CIGARETTES

LUKE ASHTON, THIS MUST BE THE PLACE, SYDNEY, AUSTRALIA

We would have called this 'Cigarettes & Coffee', after the Otis Redding song, but Luke lives upside down in Australia, so we'll let him off. He opened his bar with Charlie Ainsbury a few years ago in a city known for its classic cocktails. But This Must Be the Place is a light and airy space with spritz-style drinks. It was a refreshing addition to the scene and it has been rightly named the best bar in Sydney. Luke stresses the importance of a lightly roasted coffee bean here, as opposed to an espresso roast: something you would use for a pour-over is perfect. It lets the brighter side of coffee shine, and makes for a delicate aperitif.

Coffee bean gin

- 300ml/12oz London dry gin (Luke uses Beefeater)
- 16g/2½ tbsp lightly roasted whole coffee beans
- Kilner jar or similar airtight, non-reactive container, at least 500ml/20oz
- Funnel
- Coffee filter
- Sterilised bottle, at least 500ml/20oz

To bottle

- 300ml/12oz coffee bean gin
- 125ml/5oz Lillet Blanc
- 125ml/5oz Aperol
- 150ml/6oz Campari
- 100ml/4oz amaretto (we use Disaronno)
- 200ml/8oz water

- Jug, at least 1 litre/40oz
- 5 glass bottles, 200ml/8oz each (reusing bottles that have held tonic water or other mixers is ideal, or just use 1 larger bottle)

TO MAKE THE COFFEE BEAN GIN *1.* Pour the gin into the Kilner jar and add the coffee beans. *2.* Seal the jar and leave to infuse for 24 hours. You can leave it longer if you want a stronger coffee flavour to come through, but any more than 48 hours and the gin will start to taste extremely bitter. *3.* Strain through a coffee filter into the bottle (see p12). Seal and store in the freezer. It will keep for 1 month.

TO BOTTLE *1.* Add all the ingredients to the jug and stir to mix together. *2.* Transfer the cocktail into each of the small bottles and put the caps on. *3.* Now just get them in the freezer until they are properly chilled. They will keep in the freezer for 6 months.

GLASS SERVE Pour 200ml/8oz cocktail into a rocks glass. You can garnish with an orange twist if you're feeling fancy.

173

WARM MILK

The comfort of warm milk takes us all back to childhood, for obvious reasons. This version adds a splash of cognac to provide some of the comfort we need as adults. Make sure you don't overheat the milk: once it goes over a certain temperature its sweetness disappears. Best before bedtime on a cold winter night – this recipe serves two.

To batch

- 400ml/16oz whole milk
- 2.5g/scant tsp frankincense
- 5g/2 tsp camomile
- 100ml/4oz cognac – we like Merlet Brothers blend
- Digital cooking thermometer

BATCH *1.* Put the milk, frankincense and camomile in a saucepan on a low heat and warm gently. Use the thermometer and don't let it go above 70ºC/158ºF – so no bubbles, just a little steam off the top. ***2.*** Cover and leave to infuse on a very low heat for 5 minutes. ***3.*** Take off the heat and pour in the cognac.

GLASS SERVE Ladle from the pan into heavy glasses, which you can preheat with hot water.

TIP Try it with different spices – cinnamon, nutmeg, cardamom or cloves, for example.

MULLED
SYRUP

Mulled wine – or cider – is the scent of Christmas. The nostalgia of a large pot sitting on the hob for hours, bubbling away, with aromas drifting through the house and mixing with the fragrant tree and spiced candles… that's the fantasy, at least. The reality is often artificially flavoured wine with over-stewed spices – heating red wine for a long period will concentrate the tannins, and this, along with over-extraction of the aroma compounds from the spices, is the reason it often needs so much sugar, just to balance the drink.

Another problem with mulled wine, for a bar especially, is wastage – bartenders can't predict how much they're going to sell, and they often have to pour away leftovers. So they make it with cheap wine, and have to use even more sugar to mask its flavour. No thanks!

We prefer the idea of using a mulled syrup as a base, creating something consistent that will last a couple of weeks over the Christmas period. It gives you so much control over the intensity of the flavour, it needs much less sugar and you can use a fairly decent wine. It also means that with one stock syrup you can make mulled red wine, mulled cider or even mulled white wine.

Mulled syrup

− 3g/1½ tsp cloves
− 5g/2 scant tsp frankincense
− 1g/½ tsp ground cinnamon
− Pinch ground nutmeg
− 1 whole star anise
− 10g/½oz orange peel
− 5g/¼oz lemon peel
− 300ml/12oz decent white wine − but not too expensive
− 50g/2oz honey
− 300g/12oz caster (superfine) sugar

− Funnel
− Coffee filter
− Bowl, at least 500ml/20oz
− Sterilised bottle, at least 500ml/20oz

To serve

− 25ml/1oz mulled syrup per serve
− 100ml/4oz light red or full-bodied white wine, or dry
  cider per serve
− Orange zests, to garnish

TO MAKE THE MULLED SYRUP *1.* Put all the spices, the peel and the wine in a pan and cover with a lid. *2.* Heat on a very low heat for an hour, then take off the heat and leave to infuse in the pan for 3 hours with the lid on. This allows the spices to release their flavour without losing too much liquid to evaporation. The syrup will thicken slightly. Alternatively, cook sous vide for 30 minutes at 60°C/140°F (see p12). Leave to cool. *3.* Strain through a coffee filter into a bowl (see p12). *4.* Add the honey and sugar to the infused wine and stir to dissolve. *5.* Pour into the bottle, seal and store in the fridge for up to 3 weeks (you'll probably use it quicker though).

GLASS SERVE *1.* Put as many servings of the syrup and wine or cider as you need into a pan. *2.* Heat to your desired temperature: 60–70°C/140–158°F is about right. *3.* Ladle into glasses or mugs. *4.* Zest a bit of orange over each with a fine grater.

TIP The syrup is superb poured over vanilla ice cream for a lighter festive dessert.

SCOTTISH COFFEE

This is a Scottish riff on the famous Irish whiskey with fat-washed Scotch and shortbread-infused cream. We have this on Christmas Eve – it's a wonderful nightcap.

Buttered Scotch

– 100g/4oz salted butter
– 500ml/20oz blended Scotch whisky
– 150g/6oz caster (superfine) sugar
– Tupperware-type container or bowl, at least 1 litre/40oz
– Funnel
– Coffee filter
– Jug, at least 500ml/20oz
– Sterilised bottle, at least 500ml/20oz

Shortbread cream

– 200ml/8oz whole milk
– 150g/6oz shortbread biscuits
– 600ml/24oz double (heavy) cream

– Cheesecloth or clean tea towel (dish towel)

To serve

– 35ml/1½oz buttered Scotch per serve
– 100ml/4oz hot, freshly brewed coffee per serve (use a pour-over, French press or AeroPress etc.)
– 50ml/2oz shortbread cream per serve

TO MAKE THE BUTTERED SCOTCH *1.* On a medium heat, melt the butter in a pan. *2.* After 5 or so minutes, the butter will start to brown a little – watch it carefully and take it off the heat when it turns a hazelnut colour and there's a nutty aroma. *3.* Pour the whisky into the container. *4.* Pour the melted butter into the whisky and stir to combine. Cover with a lid or foil, then place in the freezer overnight. *5.* The next day the butter will have solidified. Strain it through a coffee filter into the jug (see p12).

6. Add the sugar and stir to dissolve. **7.** Pour into the bottle and seal. It will keep in the fridge for up to 1 year.

TO MAKE THE SHORTBREAD CREAM *1.* In a jug blender, blend the milk and the biscuits together, then strain through the cheesecloth into a large mixing bowl. *2.* Add the double cream and whisk until it forms soft peaks, but still has a fluidity to it. It will keep, covered, in the fridge for 48 hours.

GLASS SERVE *1.* Pour the buttered Scotch into a heavy-based wine glass. *2.* Top with the coffee. *3.* Spoon the shortbread cream onto the top of each drink.

INDEX

THANK YOU

Mum – for getting our names mixed up constantly and giving us the initial push to open the bar. But mainly for being there whenever either of us have ever needed anything!

Gemma – for actually sticking with me all these years and then moving her life down to London when we opened Three Sheets.

Helen – for being there. To pull a shift, make the aprons or clean the bar and put up with all our crap.

Rosey – for being our first member of staff and starting 'Snack Tuesdays'.

Rob – for pulling more than the odd shift, and getting rid of all the leftover gin.

Alan – for covering me while I was away and then sticking around, and for your unwavering enthusiasm.

Firaas – for finally moving back to the UK.

Pete and the guys – for building our bar.

Lu, Jess and 'Big D' Damian, Olly and all our family – for the amazing support.

Pedro's Crew – Alex 'Happy' Proudfoot, Dean 'Daytona' Potter, Jordan 'Crabman' Reid, Joe '#1' Fogerty, Mat, Rezina, Matthew 'Daddy' Robson, Martin, Jobe, Ross and of course 'Captain' Lyndon.

Trof Family – Millhouse, Harris, Chris, Kerry, Maccers, Flo, Imogen, Sophie and Joe (Henry C).

Manchester Mob – Marky, Aled, Adam & Hannah Binnersley, Biggsy, Audie, Pabsy, Nate 'Dobby' Booker and Adam (for my first tattoo).

Southern Fairies – friends in the Big Smoke – Joel, Gaz, Leon, Cocktail Kate, Tom Vernon, Tom Blay, Sean, Rob, Renaud, QuiQuiriQui Mel, 'Dr' Dan Schofield and Jake Murphy for helping us at out the bar; Rob Roy Cameron, Graham 'The Hobbit' Hallam, James and everyone I have met since moving down in 2016.

Tony, Zoe and The Drink Factory crew – for opening my eyes. *Guillaume* – for the laughs, *Marcis* – for the knowledge. *Team Termini* – for all the energy. *Stevie Martin, Matty H, Murray and Amy* at Ricks Edinburgh – for pushing me to stick behind the bar. *Beau, Jonboy, Kirby and Loudon* from the Socio days – thanks for the lack of memories. *James and the Sipsmith team* – for making me part of the family since 2011.

Haydn, Ben and Rory – for the last 15 years.

All the industry – for all the support. Without you guys we probably would have lasted 6 months – thanks for bigging us up!

Zena and everyone at Quadrille – for their dedication and patience.

Ola – for sharing our vision and taking incredible pictures. *Alex* – for his amazing styling and *Maeve* – for putting it all together.

To all our regulars and customers – thank you for coming in, playing credit card roulette from day one and giving us your money, but more importantly making the bar a special place to be.

Publishing Director Sarah Lavelle
Commissioning Editor Zena Alkayat
Editor Euan Ferguson
Designer Maeve Bargman
Photographer Ola O Smit
Prop Stylist Alexander Breeze
Production Director Vincent Smith
Production Controller Nikolaus Ginelli

Published in 2018 by Quadrille, an imprint of Hardie Grant Publishing

Quadrille
52–54 Southwark Street
London SE1 1UN
quadrille.com

Cataloguing in Publication Data: a catalogue record for this book is available from the British Library.

Text © Max and Noel Venning 2018
Photography © Ola O Smit 2018
Design © Quadrille 2018

ISBN 978–1–78713–155–2

Printed in China